Helping Children of Divorce

Helping Children of Divorce

Neal C. Buchanan and
Eugene Chamberlain

BROADMAN PRESS
Nashville, Tennessee

4249-26
ISBN: 0-8054-4926-4

Dewey Decimal Classification:306.8
Subject headings: DIVORCE//PARENT AND CHILD

Library of Congress Catalog Card Number: 81-67994
Printed in the United States of America

This book is dedicated to all the children of divorce whose lives have touched ours and to our own children—Michael, James, Galina, Barry, and Marigene—and to all other children who need the support of loving adults.

Neal and Gene

Contents

Introduction: May We Talk a Minute?

The two of us who are collaborating on this book want to tell you how it all came about. That way you will better understand what we are trying to share.

The book actually began when we were asked to help with a divorce seminar in our own church. But we weren't asked to help adults who were divorced or divorcing. We were asked to conduct sessions for elementary-age children whose parents were divorced or were in the process of divorcing.

Now that was a different game, one we had never played before. What we learned then, what we learned later in similar circumstances, what we had known before, and what we have discovered in other ways are all blended in this book.

So Who Is It For?

The book is for any adult concerned about what is happening in American families which are being or have been torn apart by today's stresses and strains. The book is especially for persons who care deeply about the children who are caught in the trauma of divorce.

Of course, we had some people particularly in mind as we thought, planned, and wrote. Check our listing to see if it includes you.

A divorced parent.

A parent considering divorce or in the process of divorce.

A schoolteacher.

A person who works with boys and/or girls in a setting such as Scouts or Campfire Girls.

A church staff member with professional responsibility for married adults.

A church staff member with responsibility for ministry to and work with children of elementary-school age.

A concerned citizen who wants to help children whose homes have been split by divorce.

Did you find yourself? If not, you may belong to one more category which we had in mind. You may simply be curious about a book on a subject which, it seems to us, doesn't appear in nearly enough books.

So What Will the Book Do?

We are deliberately avoiding the moral, doctrinal, and theological aspects of divorce. These questions must be faced by society, by churches, and by individuals. But these aspects lie outside the scope of this book. Our concern is with the fact of divorce and with the children whose lives are affected by divorce now.

We don't kid ourselves that the book will in itself do anything. We do have high hopes that it will help you to do something, something you can be excited about doing. Consider this formal statement of our purpose in writing the book:

> The purpose of this book is to provide a tool for use by persons who are serious about helping children and families in the crisis of divorce.

But How?

You are entitled to ask that question. Here is the answer: The book can help you discover or affirm insights you already have into the problems faced by children involved in divorce. In addition, we will share practical steps you can take immediately, and over the long haul, too.

For the book to be of the most help possible, we want to suggest a reading and study pattern designed to fit your particular needs.

If you are a parent, begin with chapter 1. Then proceed to chapter 2. Next read chapters 3, 4, and 5 if you are still interested. Just for curiosity, you may also wish to read chapter 6.

If you are a relative or close friend of a child whose parents are divorced or divorcing, you will want to follow the pattern suggested for parents. You may wish to pay particular attention to chapter 3.

If you are a schoolteacher, a Sunday School teacher, or a person who works regularly with boys and girls in some other setting, begin with chapter 1. Chapters 4 and 5 will probably interest you next. After that you may be most concerned with chapter 3. Then go on to chapter 2. And you may wish to read chapter 6, too.

If you are a church staff member with responsibility for boys and girls or for their parents, you will profit most from reading the chapters in the order in which they appear. Grapple hardest with chapter 6. It can help you determine a specific course of action. And it relates most closely to the Appendix we have prepared for those who wish to conduct a seminar for children of divorce.

One More Word

We have a deep conviction about the need for parents, churches, schools, and community agencies to work together. We believe that we all can. We hope this book will be a resource for that kind of mutual effort.

Did you skip the introduction to our book?

If you did, please don't skip the next few paragraphs. They can be the difference between gaining the most from reading this book and wasting your time.

Why? Because these paragraphs explain what this book can do. But the explanation is brief. Once you have read it, you will probably want to turn to the book's introduction unless you have already studied it carefully.

Here are some things which this book can do for you:

Give you solid data about the divorce picture in America today

Offer some insights into the problems faced by children of divorce and by the adults who play significant roles in the lives of these children

Provide a sounding board for ideas already knocking around in your head

Stimulate you to deeper insights and fresh ideas about how you personally can help children of divorce.

As we dealt with the data in this chapter, we were particularly conscious of some special boys and girls. We became acquainted with some of them in the seminars we conducted before we wrote the book. We met others in Sunday School and in other church groups. We came to know others in our neighborhoods. Others are dear to us because of family ties. No two are exactly alike, and each is of inestimable value. Knowing them has enriched our lives and given us insights we might never have gained without them.

For all they have done for us, we dedicate this chapter to the boys and girls we know whose needs led to the writing of this book. We hope this chapter will, through the lives of others, bring joy to the children of divorce.

The purpose of this particular chapter is, in a single phrase, to give you a picture of

1.
The Child of a Broken Home

Church workers, educators, social workers, psychologists, and psychiatrists all agree that a child does not come to school and park his personality outside the classroom door. On the contrary, his emotions come with him and must be taken into account if one expects the child to attend optimally to the task of learning. A child's feelings of self-worth, guilt, loss, and related feelings affect his ability to learn and to relate meaningfully to others.

In a recent seminar for children's workers on church staffs, one participant reported that thirty of the thirty-three children enrolled in a public school kindergarten in Oklahoma were from homes in which the parents had divorced or were separated. In 1975 for the first time in our nation's history over one million couples divorced. Records show that the number of divorces has increased in each succeeding year. It is an established fact that school-age children are much more likely to have divorced parents than ever before. In fact, one-fifth of the children in the United States grow up in one-parent households, mostly headed by once-married working women.

We aren't debating whether children from single-parent families are more prone to become maladjusted than are children from two-parent families. First of all, there is evidence on both sides of the question. Secondly, it is more helpful to look at some definitely established facts concerning children from broken homes. A recent study of preschool children conducted in Boulder, Colorado found that divorce can make children more susceptible to problems if it hits them along with other stresses.[1] Parents, once confronted with the divorce situation, want to know what life will be like for them and what they can do to make life better for themselves and their children.

No family, or individual for that matter, is exempt from the normal crises of life. When something has a significant impact upon an individual within a family, the whole family is affected. This is particularly true of the crisis of separation and loss, whether by death, by divorce, or by a child's leaving home for school or work. When someone leaves the family in any way, the whole family is affected; and even the smallest children experience a sense of loss. At these times children need even more intense attention from the surviving adult(s). Sadly, however, the adults who remain frequently have so great a personal need that often they are capable only of giving less.

As if coping with separation and loss were not enough, the person experiencing the adjustment of a divorce confronts other needs as well. For these reasons, at such a time any family needs help from persons outside its immediate circle.

Why should society (which includes all of us) focus on the needs of children of divorce? We are compelled to confront the issue of divorce and its effect on children for at least three important reasons. The first of these is the continuing high divorce rate in America. The number of children caught in the entangling and complicated web of divorce is increasing. Evidence presently available does not indicate that this trend is likely to be reversed.

The second reason for focusing on the needs of children of divorce is the high remarriage rate of divorced parents. Because of the high probability of remarriage, the one-parent family is, as a rule, a family in transition.

One might assume that remarriage has a positive effect on children since it produces two-parent families for them. This is not necessarily the case, however. In reality, remarriage doesn't produce two-parent families for the children. On the contrary, it creates stepchildren, sometimes on both sides, and introduces children to a whole new and complex set of relationships with which they must learn to cope. Unfortunately society has not yet accumulated enough systematic knowledge about steprelationships (stepchildren, stepparents, stepsiblings) to provide solid understanding of the real needs of these people.

Jessie Bernard has done a study of over 21,000 remarriages. He found that the general consensus among remarried parents seemed to be that very young as well as grown-up children tended to accept a new parent more easily than did adolescents.[2] Being thrust in the role of a stepchild does seem to add one more set of unknowns to the life of a child who may have already experienced more than his or her share of uncertainties. So, remarriage does not automatically produce two-parent families.

Divorce, like other family problems, is increasingly viewed by many in the helping professions as a group, rather than an individual, phenomenon. These persons hold that no individual family member's problems can be dealt with adequately apart from the consideration of his or her involvement with the rest of the family.

Those who help families, then, are attempting to strengthen all family members when one or more members are experiencing serious difficulties. This approach to helping families acknowledges that no single individual or agency has all of the answers. Rather, in counseling, the family is encouraged to identify its members' emotional reactions and resources that can be helpful in dealing with these reactions.

Another phenomenon in the current divorce picture is the increasing number of fathers being given custody of their children. This trend is relatively recent. Of the approximately 5.1 million single-parent families in the United States, 446,000 are headed by fathers alone. These father-alone families contain 710,000 children under the age of eighteen. About 75 percent of the father-headed families have been created by divorce or separation,[3] a significant change from earlier years when a father usually became a single parent as a result of the death of his wife. The number of families headed by fathers alone is not only increasing, it is rising more rapidly than the number headed by mothers.

One of the purposes of this book is to identify some of the needs of children of divorce that call for special attention and specific help. Once these particular needs have been identified and described, suggestions will be offered for making a concerted effort to bring the maximum amount of joy and predictability into the lives of these children who have experienced much sadness and uncertainty.

Some Children We All Know

As startling as statistics may be, they are still impersonal. They do not remain impersonal when we think of them in terms of boys and girls whose lives touch ours. The next few pages contain sketches from the lives of boys and girls whose lives have been touched by divorce. You will understand that it is necessary to change enough of each story to disguise the identities of the persons involved.

Allen

Allen is an affable and usually loving teenager. He and his mother live with his widowed grandmother. In fact, they have lived with Momma since Allen was just a year old. At that time Allen's parents, Marie and Allen Sr., came to the parting of the ways.

It would be more accurate to say that Allen's father came to the parting of the ways since it was he who walked out on the family. From the outset, Allen's parents refused to discuss the problem with anyone. Marie's parents, thrilled with their first grandchild, were scarcely aware of what was taking place until Allen Sr. disappeared for a week. He brought the car home with several thousand miles added to the odometer, announced he was leaving, packed his things, and departed.

For several days, Marie acted as if things were perfectly normal. Then she and the baby moved "home." No one ever talked about whether or not the arrangement would be permanent. In six months Marie returned to work, and Momma became her daytime stand-in.

In the early years of Allen's life, his grandfather was employed. When Pop came in from work, he was sometimes ready for a free-for-all romp with Allen. At other times, he was likely to be a stern disciplinarian, through as a rule he was permissive.

Marie found single-parenting no picnic. Although living with her parents eased the economics of her situation, the tension of being a parent to her child and a child to her parents was almost too much. As a result, Marie fluctuated in her discipline of Allen. She talked a high standard but frequently permitted flagrant disregard of that standard. Though Marie was hard on Allen from time to time, she grew defensive when either of her parents was equally severe.

When Allen began to encounter difficulties with his teacher while in the primary grades, his mother decided to place him in a private school. Her intention at the time was to return him to public school in a year or two. But as the years came and went, she found it easier to manage the private school fees than to face the problems she thought would arise in public school. In the meantime Allen became increasingly stubborn about things like telling his grandmother where he was going to spend his afternoons, getting his hair cut, following bedtime routines, and doing homework.

At thirteen, Allen is talking about dropping out of school. Whether this is an empty threat to get his own way about other things or whether he sees no hope of academic success is uncertain. When he talks about his future, he outlines lofty goals with little or no concept of what is involved in achieving his ambitions.

Allen never mentions his father. What he knows about his father remains his secret. He obviously hungers for adult male attention. He tests his uncles as if he wanted the discipline which he nastily resists when it comes.

Louisa

Louisa's checkered history is scarcely typical of children of divorce. Yet it has many things in common with all rejected children. During the first ten years of Louisa's life, her parents separated three times without any legal action. In each instance, her mother walked out—usually after a classic fight in which body blows were exchanged.

The family moved with dismaying regularity. Louisa is now a full year behind her age-mates in school and is in danger of losing another year. During a relatively stable period, Louisa was befriended by a schoolteacher who invited her to Sunday School. There Louisa found a quality of life that she did not know existed.

Recently Louisa's parents had the most severe bout of their stormy marriage. Once again her mother walked out. She found a room and initiated a suit for divorce, charging incompatibility.

Louisa remained with her father. Recently he told her that she really is not his child. He wanted her to go to her mother's sister in a distant state. Louisa, heartbroken, sought help from her Sunday School teacher, who contacted the aunt. Unfortunately, the aunt was reluctant to take Louisa into her home. She considers Louisa's mother a tramp and fears what might happen to her own marriage if her sister were to move to her town to be near Louisa.

Pat and Patience

Really it is Patrick and Patience. Patience is ten, two years older than Patrick. For the past two years they have lived with their mother, visiting with their father on weekends and sometimes during the week. He has unrestricted visiting privileges.

Both children seem well-adjusted. Each is doing well in school and generally relates well to other children and to adults in school and at church. They are both confident of their parents' love for them.

Neither of them has any idea of what drove their parents to divorce. Neither parent has ever said anything to put down the other parent. When problems require cooperative effort on the part of their father and mother, the children get a solid-front treatment. "Divide and conquer" works no better now than it did prior to the divorce.

Outsiders are impressed with the civility the divorced Andersons have maintained. Even close friends are amazed, although they always considered Al and Berta to be polished and reserved persons. They would not be surprised to discover that Patrick and Patience do not understand why two people who obviously love them and seem to bear each other no ill will are unable to live under the same roof.

Matt and Jan

Matt and Jan look like the ideal American children. Matt is dark and stocky. Who can doubt that he is destined to be an all-American? He is exactly two years older than his angelic blond sister.

Matt's dark good looks come from his mother's side, though his size is a legacy of his tall father's family. Jan resembles her father in coloring but will likely be a more petite adult than most women in her father's family.

Their parents, Jim and Mary Ann, were always a striking couple. Mary Ann's daintiness, emphasized by large black eyes, was the perfect foil for Jim's Nordic litheness. And her quiet dignity balanced his easygoing gregariousness.

Only that is not how things worked out. Jim's easygoing manner extended too easily to other women. And Mary Ann's dignity turned out to be a cool aloofness. Unable to communicate their feelings, they eventually decided to separate.

Mary Ann sees herself as an abandoned woman left to struggle with an impossible task. In spite of receiving regular and reasonable payments from Jim for child support, she considers herself his victim. Her bitterness toward Jim extends to all males—her boss, her pastor, and teachers at the school her children attend.

In fact, that bitterness extends even to Matt. She asserts that his meanness is a lot more than being "all boy." She constantly nags him—his shirttail is out; his shoe is untied; he fails to say "Yes, Ma'am"; he obeys too slowly.

But Jan is such a godsend. She is pretty, she is smart, she is mannerly, and she is clean. She is entirely satisfactory as far as her mother is concerned. Jan is also becoming a passive child, trying quietly to be the child her mother talks about.

Robert and Thad

Robert and Thad live with their father, Leonard. He has little to say about the departure of their mother. Careful to avoid being critical of her, he simply says nothing at all. Neither of the boys really knows anything of the circumstances involved in the divorce. They do know that Mother has remarried and that in many ways their stepfather is quite unlike their sober and taciturn father. They enjoy the weekends they spend with their mother and Steven. Not that they like Steven all that much, but he is fun. Leonard is serious about almost everything, and especially about doing a good job of parenting his sons. His own parents think that he tries too hard. They go along with the rules he lays down for the boys, even though the boys are actually with them more hours than they are with their father.

Both boys display the kind of manners one used to see in movies set in upper-class academies. If anything else sets them apart from other children, it is their mutual dependence. Neither is inclined to undertake anything in which the other cannot be involved. Even while doing his best with a task, each keeps watch on the other, encouraging and supporting.

Do any of these children sound familiar to you? They well may— in a general way. But they are not exactly like the children of divorce you know. This is because there is no typical child of divorce—no more than there is a typical child of any other sort. Children of divorce are, first of all, children. Their traits and characteristics are much like those of other children. Whatever may be said about children of divorce in general must be applied carefully when dealing with a particular child. With this understanding clearly in mind, let's look at

Some Common Reactions of Children to Divorce

While children of divorce come in all sizes, shapes, and temperaments, their reactions to divorce frequently bear strong resemblance. If one were to list all of the reactions he has seen on the part of a thousand children of divorce, he would have a paper of staggering length. If the reactions were placed on a line in an order ranging from the slightest observable reaction to the most overt action, the line would go from here to the horizon. But if those reactions were to be placed in categories, the majority of the reactions could be classified in one of the eight categories we are going to consider.

Before we take a look at the categories, here is a caution: A single child may in the process of adjusting to the divorce of his parents have any, all, or none of these reactions.

Second caution: There is no certain sequence in which a child will experience these reactions.

Third caution: Just because a child's emotional life has been dominated for a time by one of these reactions does not ensure that he is finished with that reaction once and for all. In all likelihood, he will bounce from reaction to reaction and back again. The order in which he experiences these reactions is determined in part by his own makeup and in part by the attitudes and actions of the persons who play significant roles in his life.

Caution four: A child may have one or more of these reactions simultaneously. He is not abnormal because he, for instance, develops an intense dislike for both the parent who has stayed with him and for the parent who has left the home.

With these cautions clearly in mind, let's examine eight common reactions of children to divorce. To save your thumbing through the next few pages, here they are in a single listing: being physically ill; feeling guilty; not caring; pretending all is well; hoping for remarriage; being confused; hating the parent with whom he lives; and hating the parent who has left him.

Being Physically Ill

Anyone who works with children—or adults, for that matter—knows that physical illness is a common reaction of a body under continuing stress. Regardless of how amiably his parents behave, nearly any child is intensely upset by the dissolution of his home. He lives in stress through the period of increasing tension, through the period of separation, and through the period of adjustment. And his body is quite likely to react.

If this reaction comes as a tummy ache, even the rankest amateur is likely to spot the cause. A headache may be equally obvious. Folk wisdom says that under stress the part of the body which is already the weakest or most cantankerous is likely to act up. That bit of lore may not be the best medical advice, but it underscores something we need to remember. A child whose parents are experiencing extreme difficulties is quite likely to become physically ill.

One reason it is important to remember this reaction is that one may be tempted to call the child a goldbrick. He is not.

On the other hand, one may be tempted to treat the illness as if it had only a physical cause. Obviously a strep throat must be treated; so must a stumped toe. But the underlying cause also requires treatment or, at the very least, recognition. Stress can be reduced by being recognized and accepted as normal.

Feeling Guilty

When told that children frequently react to divorce by feeling guilty, many adults are surprised. "But it isn't his fault," exclaimed one mother. "It is his father and I who are guilty."

We can better understand a child's sense of guilt if we recall our own childhood. Maybe you never resented your mother or father or brother or sister, but most of us did at one time or another. We wished something dreadful would happen to that person. The nature of that dreadful thing varied with our age and with the person toward whom we felt hostile.

Most of the times when we had such feelings, nothing at all happened. In a few hours or a few days, we forgot our negative feelings.

But perhaps something bad did happen. When the person we momentarily disliked suffered physical pain or emotional distress, we were shocked. Look what we had done! With childhood's easy belief in magic, we saw cause and effect at work. We wished Mama ill and presto! She dropped her best china platter on the kitchen floor. We brought on the disaster; we were guilty.

Now imagine the feelings a child must grapple with when his parents shatter the home he thinks of as right and normal. Adults are good, adults are strong, adults can cope. If they have been overtaken by disaster, it must be the result of the bad thought the child has harbored against them. The divorce is his fault.

A group of children was listening to a story about a girl who felt guilty because of her parents' divorce. "That's the way I felt," one girl suddenly exclaimed. "I still feel that way a lot of the time." After her fervent outburst, other children in the group began to share their feelings. Most of them explained that they, too, had felt guilty about their parents' separation and divorce.

Some of the children told how their parents had recognized their feeling and attempted to help them. In some cases this help consisted mainly of an explanation that the child didn't need to feel guilty, that no one was actually guilty. This level of reassurance didn't seem to help a great deal. One child said, "I still felt guilty."

The child who feels guilty does need reassurance that he has not caused the divorce. Within the limits of his understanding, he probably needs to be told something of the real facts of the case. Such a statement may be as simple as: "Your mother and father were no longer happy living together. We decided it would be better to live apart. So you see, we would have divorced no matter what you did." The child does not, of course, need a full description of the high crimes of the absent partner.

The child will continue to need this sort of reassurance from time to time. One telling is not enough, as dramatic as may be its effect at the moment.

The child also needs to understand that his feeling is not abnormal. The feeling is common among children of divorce, and it reflects a common feeling of adults involved in divorce. One man in his mid-thirties said of his own divorce: "The hardest part was telling my parents. There had never been a divorce in our family. I felt so guilty."

Not Caring

Nearly everyone loves the story of the making of a pearl. A bit of grit, an effort to protect the body from irritation, and the oyster gradually builds an object of great beauty.

A similar mechanism works in the life of a person injured in spirit. In some instances great beauty may be produced, but the more common result is not nearly so happy. A child traumatized by the separation and divorce of his parents may protect himself from further hurt by simply not caring what happens within the family. Not caring may protect the person, but it does not necessarily produce great beauty.

We often tell ourselves that the child who says or acts as if he does not care is covering up a deep disturbance. We may try to get him to admit that he really does care and to cry out his hurt. But we may be wrong. He may truly be indifferent.

Not caring spreads dangerously. The child who ceases to care what happens to the people dearest to him can also cease to care what happens to himself.

Pretending All Is Well

Another common reaction to divorce is pretending that nothing has been changed. If one asks a number of children, "How has divorce changed your life?" one is likely to get some bland stares.

"Well, not really," may be accompanied by a shrug.

The child is not, in a sense, lying to you. He is protecting himself from hurt by pretending that nothing has been significantly altered by the dramatic events of his life. He can do such a good job of pretending that he believes himself.

A child of divorce can usually count a number of things about his life which are not changed, at least not on the surface. He still goes to the same school. He still goes to the same church. He still has the same room at home, plays with the same children, and pets the same cats and dogs. He still plays on the same soccer or football team, or still takes piano lessons. He is still loved by the same parents, even though they are no longer a matched pair.

Small wonder, then, if he pretends that nothing significant is changed. No wonder he acts as if he does not understand why others treat him as if his world has fallen apart.

Hoping for a Rematch

A twelve-year-old girl was talking with a teacher in a church setting. "I have a question," she said. "Would it be all right according to the Bible if my daddy left the woman he has married and came back and married my mother?"

The teacher realized that the girl was not posing a theological or doctrinal problem. She was not interested in the morality of the situation or even in what the teachings of Jesus might be on the subject.

She was really crying out, "Is there any hope that my daddy and mother will remarry and we will be a family again?"

The teacher was wise enough to talk with her about her real question, and he was honest with her. There was no hope for a rematch.

Regardless of how peculiar his home situation is, a young child tends to accept it as normal. Even when his parents have brought harm and disruption into his life, a child usually feels more secure with his parents together than with them separated. The hope that his divorced parents will remarry persists in many cases long, long after all actual possibility of such an arrangement has faded away.

Being Confused

Who is surprised that a child is confused by divorce? No thoughtful person. But we still may be insensitive to the depth of the child's bewilderment. We may be inclined to interpret his confused conduct as plain orneriness.

The confused child may one moment long for his parents to remarry. In such moments he thinks more of an idealized situation than of the situation which actually existed prior to the divorce.

The next moment he may be afraid that the marriage will be mended. In that moment he recalls the fighting and the bitter words which poisoned his days and nights.

Sometimes he may think that running away from home is a solution for his hurt. Yet he is desperately afraid of losing what he has managed to hold onto.

He may feel sorry for either his mother or his father at one moment. Shortly his sympathy has reversed.

In all likelihood his parents are also going through a lot of confusion. Even the other significant persons who surround the child may be confused about their feelings. They may abhor divorce and wish the child's parents were together again. At the same time, they may be relieved that the relationship is ended and dread to think what the actual situation would be were the marriage to be restored.

Hating the Parent Who Has Custody

"All she does is nag me. I wish I could go live with my father. He sure doesn't treat me like she does." The speaker was an eleven-year-old boy.

The listening adult had heard the remark many times before. Sometimes it had been said with less intensity, but the sentiment was not all that different. A child of divorce frequently feels strong resentment, even active hate, toward the parent who has custody of him.

There may be several reasons for this feeling, though the feeling may persist even if the apparent reasons are systematically eliminated. Let's consider some of the obvious reasons.

First of all, the parent with custody has to handle alone the difficult task of disciplining a distressed child. And he has to administer this discipline during a time in his own life when he may have the least emotional reserve. The parent with custody, as a rule, also has to earn all or at least a major part of the money needed by the family. Facing the work world, plus facing the chores of running a household, can push even the strongest and most balanced person toward the edge. Viewed from an objective vantage, a child of such a parent may have legitimate cause for complaint.

Second, the child can scarcely avoid comparing the treatment he receives from each of his parents. The parent with visiting privileges may overindulge the child in order to avoid conflict when they are together. This easy approach contrasts sharply with day-in-day-out holding-the-line-through-thick-and-thin.

Hating the Parent Who Is Gone

In contrast to the child who was so upset by his custodial parent's treatment of him is the child who venomously spat out: "I don't care if my dad never comes back. I hate him."

Did this child really mean what he said? Some tell us that *hate* is a strong word for a child's negative feelings. But the boy certainly did sound as if he knew what he was saying and meant every word of it.

Behind his words may have been the conviction that his father was the cause of all the trouble. In the boy's opinion, Dad should have stayed with them no matter what. Tied to that opinion was the dreadful feeling that his father had walked out because he did not love the boy.

From that point it is easy for a child to move back to guilt. If someone you love doesn't love you, what is wrong with you? What awful thing have you done that caused the loss of love?

With such a cauldron of feelings it is no wonder that a child hates the absent parent. His hate may persist in spite of its lack of basis in fact. It may also persist in spite of kind treatment by the absent parent, or even in the face of overindulgence.

There they are: eight common reactions of children to divorce. As you considered each of them, you probably thought of one or more children you know who are experiencing these reactions. You may be familiar enough with one child to trace the presence of each of these reactions in his period of adjustment to the divorce of his parents.

Some of the Major Problems Created for the Child

Love and Acceptance

Many of the problems all children face relate to feeling love and acceptance. It is not enough for us as parents to tell our children that we love them—although this is needful. Children have to feel love and acceptance. We communicate this feeling to them more by what we do than by what we say. To a child, an attitude is considered a fact. Thus, if a child (or an adult for that matter) does not feel loved, that lack of love becomes a fact for him. It becomes increasingly clear, then, that if we are unwilling to take the actions necessary to communicate love and concern, we can forget about the words. After all is said and done, we only believe that which we do. Children know that.

Children also know instinctively that the most basic of all human needs is the need to be loved—the need to feel that one matters to others, one is valued by others, one is important to others. Oh, a child may not be able to put this awareness into words; nevertheless, it is intuitive knowledge that he possesses. The reason this feeling of being loved is so important is that it is the foundation on which one's view of himself is built. And how one views himself is of major significance in determining his adjustment to life. Since the home is essentially where this view is developed, it is also the place with the greatest potential for giving the child the message that he is not loved. So the children of divorce, already experiencing a lack of love between mother and father, need especially to feel that they are loved. How do you meet this need? Specific suggestions will be offered at the end of this chapter.

Anger

Another problem with which children of divorce have to deal is anger. Whether they can express it in these terms or not, most children of divorce are angry because their parents will not get married again. As long as children do not understand the finality of divorce, they continue to cling to the false hope that their parents will change their minds.

Their anger is a problem to these children because, like other children, they learned from an early age that anger will often get them what they want. Temper tantrums and other expressions of anger have resulted in the children's getting their way. Since they want mother and father to get married again, it is only natural that children of divorce try one of the most successful techniques they know for getting their way.

It is helpful for adults to recognize that children have these anger feelings. And it is not wrong for a child to feel this way. By not blaming the child for something he cannot help (his feelings of anger), the adult has taken the first step in helping the child deal constructively with his anger.

Guilt

It is extremely common for children to feel, in addition to anger, a great deal of guilt over mother and daddy's divorce. From the child's point of view, he is the one responsible for the divorce. For this reason, children will often begin to make all kinds of promises to their parents if they will not get a divorce. They may say such things as, "I'll be good," "I'll do better in school," or, "I will not ask for the bicycle any more." All of these statements indicate that, in one way or another, the child feels the divorce is his fault and that he can do something which will make the situation different. A wise and understanding parent will exercise a great deal of patience at this point. Both parents, ideally, need to help the child gradually come to the realization that the divorce is definitely not his fault, and that he is still loved by both parents.

Peer Criticism

Having dealt with the feelings of guilt within the family, one of the first obstacles a child will face outside the home is peer criticism or chiding. Children are often forthrightly candid and cruelly blunt in the comments they make to other children. Children whose parents are not divorced sometimes make fun of children from divorced homes. They may think that children of divorce are different, and they may not want to play with children whose parents are divorced. However, in communities in which divorce is common, such attitudes are not likely to prevail.

It may be helpful to point out to a child that all of us get our feelings hurt from time to time. The child should be reminded that just because someone else says or thinks something about him doesn't make it true. It may be that person's way of trying to deal with some problems of his own. The best way to deal with people who are behaving this way is to be your natural self. If you are friendly with other people, most of them will be friendly with you. The fact that one's parents are divorced, others will discover, has nothing to do with the kind of person you are.

Jealousy

Children whose parents are divorced often feel unhappy because other children around them have parents who are still married. They may feel that few children are like them—living with only one parent. They can get to know other children of divorced parents through church groups, community organizations, or clubs for divorced persons. Through activities in these organizations, children will often learn from one another. Too, they will become aware of the fact that many children are living in homes in which the parents are divorced.

One way that a parent who retains custody sometimes tries to help a child feel less badly about the loss of the parent who is no longer present is by seldom, if ever, mentioning the parent who is gone. There is a maxim which says that the only thing worse than speaking ill of the dead is not speaking of the dead at all. In a real sense the child is grieving over the loss of a parent through divorce in a way which is similar to grieving over a loss through death. Trying to ignore this fact will not make the loss less painful. On the contrary, being able to talk about it is extremely desirable. Such discussion should be encouraged, especially during the first few weeks and months of the divorce. Incidentally, this kind of talking may help the parent as much as the child.

What Does This Mean for Me?

As each person—reader or writer—looks at himself and the children of divorce, he wants to know what is best for the children. Each of us asks, "How can I help these children—my own and children of others—have the best that can be offered?" The next paragraph could be your answer.

First, I recognize a principle of life that much can be done if many are willing each to do a little. The one resource which will make the difference in the lives of multitudes of children is the one with which all are equally endowed—time. *How much do I value children?* The answer to this big question may be hidden in this simple question: How much time do I have for children—my own and others?

Time and love are one and the same with children. We may not mean to deprive a child of love, but if we have no time for him, he interprets it exactly that way. Each chapter of this book offers suggestions for making life better for children, especially for children of divorce. Often the answer for a given child is as simple as a caring individual who is willing to make an investment of time. This kind of gift in all probability will be the greatest contribution many of us will ever make to society.

Bruno Bettelheim, a man who dedicated his life to helping children with severe emotional problems, wrote a book entitled *Love Is Not Enough*. While love may not be all that children need, it is far ahead of whatever is in second place. The title of Bettelheim's book, however, implies that children do have other important needs. These, too, will be considered in the chapters which follow.

"I have thirty-two children in my room this year. Of that number, twenty-seven are from homes in which only one of the natural parents presently lives with the children." This comment was made by a public-school teacher following a workshop we conducted for the faculty of her school. This teacher and many others like her are confronted daily with many parents who have already experienced divorce or are in the process of separation or divorce.

Some children have only one parent because of death. Whatever the reason, the loss to the child is very real. Church-school teachers and leaders know these same parents and their children. We should all try to better understand how we can meet the needs of these children and their parents.

It is not easy to be a parent. It has never been easy to be a parent. One has to be a parent to appreciate this fact. Being an only parent, though, is even more difficult. This chapter focuses on the parents and the difficulties they face—the full-time parent and the part-time. Specific suggestions come from our experience in working with public-school teachers, church-school teachers, people in the helping professions, and

2.
Parents
of the Child
# of a Broken
Home

It is not easy to be a parent, even when conditions are ideal and two people are sharing the responsibility. But when much of the responsibility is being carried by one person, under conditions which are less than ideal, then you do not have to be a Ph.D. to understand that the job is tough. This chapter addresses some of the major problems of parents.

It is our sincere belief that most parents—whether divorced or living together—want to do what is best for their children. Knowing what is best for your child is not always easy. For this reason, we have attempted to identify some of the major problem areas for divorced parents. Next, the focus is on problems of the parent who stays. Finally, we have identified some of the problems faced by the parent who is no longer in the home with the child.

Based on the previously stated belief that most parents want to do what is best for their child, specific suggestions have been offered to parents as they relate to the problems which have been identified and discussed. At the end of the chapter suggestions are offered to both parents.

Problems Common to Both

A Time of Reappraisal

This book assumes that the worst has happened. It doesn't address itself to what might have been done to save the marriage. The main thrust is how one can make the best of one's situation after divorce has occurred. Once the divorce is a reality, what is one to do? Should one try to forget the past as if it were a bad nightmare? Does one secretly nurse a bitterness which will later reveal itself in his own behavior as well as his child's? This may be the case if one tries to go along as though nothing had happened.

Although counseling may not have been sought before the marriage ended, it almost assuredly should be after the marriage has ended. There are important questions to ask such as, What went wrong? Where do I go from here? Is life worth living? How did I fail?

One may try to argue with himself, *But I was not the one to blame. Everyone knows that I did not leave with another man (or woman).* While we may not view ouselves as being at fault, it is nevertheless helpful to do a soul-searching reappraisal. Most often this is best done in the presence of someone else who can help us see ourselves as others see us. Human nature being what it is, we may carry a heavier load of self-righteousness than we realize. We protect ourselves from our own criticism by becoming convinced that our emotional problems are due to external circumstances to which we can point with some degree of accuracy. We cannot see the extent to which our own strong feelings affect our interpretation of those outward circumstances. Thus, one of the surest signs of emotional maturity is our willingness to say to someone else, "I need your help."

Help is often found in the person of a pastor, a counselor, or a friend who has a sympathetic ear. Taking the initiative to seek this kind of counsel may be difficult and painful, but it demonstrates maturity.

One of the best definitions of maturity we have is by an anonymous author who said: "Maturity is the growing awareness that you are neither wonderful or hopeless. It has been said to be the making of peace between what is and what might be. It isn't a destination; it is a road. It is the moment you realize that something you have long believed in isn't so, and, parting with the old conviction, find that you are still you. It is the moment you discover somebody can do your job as well as you can, and you go on doing it anyway. It is the moment you realize you are forever alone but so is everybody else, and so in some way you are more together than ever. Maturity is a hundred other moments when you find out who you are. It is letting life happen in its own good order and making the most of what there is." Maturity is counting the value and the cost and choosing the value regardless of the cost.

In making a satisfactory adjustment to divorce, the first obstacle to overcome is the inability to acknowledge that the failure of one's marriage is in some way one's own fault. If one is able to admit that at least part of the fault is one's own, then he benefits in two important ways. First of all, he is in a much better position to discuss the divorce with increased freedom and objectivity. Being able to talk about the marriage and its failure reduces the amount of grief, guilt, and sadness associated with this personal crisis.

The second benefit is to the child or children. Most parents really want to do what is best for their children. The fact that you are reading this book is evidence of your desire to make life better for your child. When there is a willingness to acknowledge that neither parent is completely without fault, then there is less need for a parent to defend himself to the child. The parent realizes that he does not need to defend himself to the child at the expense of the other parent.

The immediate help for the child is that he is not put in the unfair position of having to choose between the parents. Probably the more important lesson for the child is that his parents are decent people. They do not find it necessary to engage in bickering, name-calling, or humiliating one another. From this experience he may further conclude that it is possible to disagree with someone without attacking that person or violating his dignity as a fellow human being. In too many families, apparently, the parting of father and mother is on much less amiable terms.

How to Treat the Past

When trying to decide how to treat the past, one of the first problems facing a divorced parent is how to talk about the other parent. We have already offered some suggestions on how to do this. Having touched upon this important area of communication, let's focus on the area of feeling. The child needs to have some emotional assurance that father and mother will both continue to care for him and to love him. Further, he needs to know that mother and father will have respect for one another. Giving this kind of support is never easy and may be impossible in some situations.

Remember that whenever words are communicated to children, more than the words is communicated. Children pick up their parents' feelings so easily that a "feelings" message is always communicated along with the words. If the child is experiencing grief or some other emotion relating to the divorce, it is good if he can also pick up the fact that his feelings are genuinely shared, and that all of the family members are interested in one another's lives and will continue this caring relationship. Thus, one of the first things to remember about the past is that the quarreling and bickering of the past should remain there. If a parent loves his child and is concerned for his emotional health, he will refrain from displaying hostility toward the other parent or from making disparaging remarks about him or her.

Another way to treat the past is to put the anger of the past behind you. Anger should not be allowed to sap present energy or obscure hope for success in the future. It is easier to talk about putting anger behind us than it is to do it. One reason is that anger is deceitful. It often masquerades as something else. For example, anger is closely akin to depression. And depression is on the increase. The 70's were referred to by many as the decade of depression. There is little prospect, as far as we can tell, that the 80's or beyond will bring any decrease in depression. The best advice in the world concerning anger is still, "Be ye angry, and sin not: let not the sun go down upon your wrath" (Eph. 4:26). Depression which is allowed to accumulate from day to day becomes a burden that even the strongest cannot bear.

Separate Residency

Having taken a hard look at one's own part in the breakup of a marriage, one of the first problems divorced parents face is that of establishing separate residences. Formal legal actions relating to divorce often cannot be initiated until this step has been taken. One does not have to be an expert in economics to understand that this arrangement is more expensive than sharing a common residence. This means that less money is available for personal needs of the parents and children than before the divorce. This is no small concern when one realizes that, contrary to popular opinion, divorce occurs more often among lower-income families than among the well-to-do families. William Goode established this fact in a study he conducted in 1956.[1]

Grief

Because a family is a caring fellowship, it is not surprising to find that when a marriage is terminated through divorce, the partners will have to deal with the grief process in their lives. We have talked about the process of grief which the children experience, but we need also to think about how the parents handle their grief. If you as a parent have not dealt with your grief relating to the divorce, you are not going to be of much help to your child in this area. One does not deal with grief by ignoring it or hoping that it will go away. While the divorce may be in the past, the grief continues to be felt in the present for a length of time which will vary from couple to couple and individual to individual.

How, then, does one deal with grief so that it can become a part of the past and not continue to interfere with adequate functioning in the present? The first step is to acknowledge its presence and not try to pretend that it isn't there. Many persons who have experienced divorce say that this kind of a break in a relationship is more difficult to deal with than if the partner had died. Research in the area of grief has revealed that people usually go through several phases, including: shock; numbness of feeling; a struggle between fantasy and reality; periods of despair and depression; and finally the development of new interests and the transfer of love to new objects.

When a person is trying to deal with a significant loss, his initial feeling is usually shock or numbness. Many people complain that they don't feel anything and experience guilt. It is normal, then, to feel shock or guilt.

The next stage in the grief process is the fight between fantasy and reality. For example, the person who is bereaved or is experiencing grief wants to believe that the loss has not occurred (fantasy), but reality keeps confronting the individual and eventually wins. The sooner one is able to accept the loss, the better one is able to deal with it.

When reality wins, whether in a divorce or a death situation, the heavy impact of the loss occurs and the individual begins his most severe period of bereavement. The flood of grief may be expressed in weeping, talking, withdrawal, or some other form of behavior. During this time the person experiencing the grief needs someone to be a good listener, to be present, to be available.

As the flood of grief begins to subside, one experiences selective memory—often accompanied by stabbing pain. The bereaved person will select certain memories connected with the one who has departed and will experience both emotional and physical pain.

The final stage in the normal grief process is the development of new interests and the transfer of love to new objects. One will not have worked through the grief process successfully until there is a reinvestment of oneself in new objects and activities. If this stage is achieved too quickly, one may be attempting to bypass the other stages of grief because they are painful. This is like trying to ignore the grief; it does not work.

Because of the individual differences of people and their different experiences, individuals move through these five stages of grief differently and at different rates.[2] Most people who have someone in whom they can confide will be able to manage the grief process successfully. If, given the proper time, a person is unable to move from one stage to another, professional help is usually needed.

A Tendency to Blame the Other

Without minimizing the effect of divorce on adults, one must remember that children are the ones whose lives are most affected by divorce. We underscore an observation made by many in the fields of counseling, the ministry, and the legal profession. In most divorce proceedings there is a tendency on the part of one parent (and sometimes both parents) not just to blame the other parent, but to teach a child to hate the other parent.

In the book *Marriage Happiness or Unhappiness*, Tom R. Blaine shared his experiences as a trial judge in more than ten thousand divorce cases. He said, "If I had to name one unpardonable sin of a parent toward his child it would be the act of one parent trying to make a child hate the other."[3]

In other parts of the world, as well as here in the United States, we have seen the tragic results of children being taught to hate. This happens at such an early age in some cultures that it almost appears that the children are born with a hatred toward those whom the adults hate. Yet, from recent child development research we know that prejudice, for example, is practically unknown in children before age three. Obviously, children learn prejudice and hatred from those who are closest to them—usually their parents. These prejudicial attitudes have a far-reaching effect upon the lives of children.

It is difficult to realize the harm that can be done to a child by teaching him to hate anyone, especially a parent. While mother and father will feel strongly about some things that have happened in the past, they must realize that this is their problem and not the child's.

There will be the ever-present temptation to make the other parent appear to be at fault and possibly be looked upon with scorn and contempt. There is a fallacy in this kind of thinking, however. It is ultimately self-defeating. It is a boomerang; the parent who throws hatred and unkindness out will have it come back to him. A hard lesson for parents to learn, it seems, is that alienating the affection of a child from the other parent eventually leads to the child's despising the parent for so doing. A child does hold it against a parent who tries to make him dislike the other parent.

That one must give vent to his feeling of ill will against a former mate is understandable. But what is not understandable or desirable is the thoughtlessness of a parent who uses a small child as the channel for expressing hatred for the child's other parent. We are not suggesting that one be self-degrading or that one assume a martyr complex about the past. We do suggest that one be objective enough to realize that there may have been fault on both sides. This will not be far from the truth. Even if a parent feels that all the fault was on the other side, nothing is gained by trying to communicate this point of view to the child. On the contrary, one may do harm to the child by taking such a stance.

You may be asking, "Well, how do I discuss my former wife or former husband with my child?" There is little need to discuss your feelings about your former mate with your child. However, you should not deny your child the right to talk about his other parent with you. If he lives with the other parent and you deny him the opportunity of talking about that parent, then you are depriving him of discussing his daily experiences with you. If, for instance, a child lives with his mother, it would be foolish and cruel to give him the feeling that it is wrong to talk about her. A child cannot deny his situation; if he is dependent on his mother, the father should accept that as a fact. A simple way you can avoid talking about her, yourself, is to focus on the activity your child mentions, rather than on the people involved.

If your child tells you that he or she has messages from your ex-wife or ex-husband, tell your son or daughter that you will contact your ex yourself for a direct message. When communicating with your child, be careful with both compliments and criticisms of one's ex-mate. As we pointed out, if you as father criticize your child's mother, you are hurting your child. If, on the other hand, you compliment her excessively, you may be giving your child the message that he is not to trust what you say. After all, he may reason, "If Dad thinks Mom is so great, why didn't they stay together?"

More Need to Show Love to Child

Aside from money, separate residency deprives the child of other things which money cannot buy, such as the presence of the parent with whom he is no longer living. For most children, this means that the absent parent is the father. The mother is now faced with the problem of trying to be both mother and father. Since much of what children learn from parents is through modeling, it becomes a problem for a mother to provide the male identification which a boy needs. Too, there is increasing evidence that in order to learn how to relate properly to members of the opposite sex, girls need a man (ideally, the father) to whom they can relate in a meaningful way. We are not sure of all that is involved in this kind of relationship, but some girls who miss it apparently feel the need to get the affection and attention of members of the opposite sex in socially unaccepted ways.

As parents, we should have long ago put aside the Freudian fears of openly demonstrating love for our children of the opposite sex. More problems are likely to result when we fail to express our love for them.

Most Difficult Developmental Period for Child of Divorce

Divorce or separation does not register with this kind of impact if a child is an infant through the age of three. Sex differences are not important to very young children, and they do not need a particular sex-role model to any significant degree.

From ages three to six, however, the child needs both parents more than during any other period in life. At this stage of development, children have intimate feelings toward the parent of the opposite sex. These feelings need to be counterbalanced and modified by association with both parents. The absence of a mother or father during this three-to-six age period of growth is probably the most difficult time for the child.

The reason we take time to talk about this period more is that if a child can be helped through this developmental stage successfully, then there is a greater likelihood that he can master the important task of developing good relationships with others. Do we need to be reminded that childhood is not a time set aside for adults to finish God's work? Rather, childhood is a time when parents cooperate with God by helping a child along a joyful journey—a journey which should not be rushed. One cannot change a child's rate of growth without tragic consequences.

The four-year-old is at the expansive age. This is the uninhibited, out-of-bounds age. His mind is fluid. It seems to flow from one thing to another. Whatever he does may seem laughable, but he is not to be laughed at.

It is quite normal for a four-year-old to use "four-letter words." If we appear shocked at his language, he may take this as an invitation to repeat these words again and again. One of the best ways to deal with bad language at this age is to cut off the child's source of knowledge. This may mean that a parent has to be more selective in choosing playmates and others with whom the child associates.

At this age, the child often says, "Watch me." He wants and needs adults who will take the time to observe his newfound skills, praise him for tiny successes, and assure him that he is "growing up" in every way. He may not have a comparable period in his life when success will be as important to him.

By four and one-half, the child is in the "fitting together" stage. He is trying to separate fact from fiction. It is at this age that children have some understanding of death, but they still do not understand death's permanence. Neither do children understand the permanence of divorce when it occurs at this time.

Age five is a relatively calm and smooth stage. The five-year-old is sometimes described as being in a "stuck pattern." He has to complete himself with someone else. He gets and wants adult approval. Our wish for all children is that they have both parents to relate to during this significant period of three through six.

Problems of the Parent Who Stays

The mother is the parent who still gets custody of the child in most divorce proceedings. The assumption is, then, that the comments in this section of the chapter will be addressed primarily to mothers. It should be noted, though, that times are changing. More fathers are now seeking custody of their children. This is due, in part, to a revolution in our definitions of male and female roles. Men are taking a more active role in child rearing. This is no longer the exclusive domain of mothers. Because of this more active involvement on the part of many fathers, they are no longer content to assume the role of "weekend" father simply because their marriage has ended. An increasing number of fathers are gaining full or joint custody of their children.

Not only is the role of the father changing, but also we have seen in recent years a considerable liberalization of divorce laws. Many states are moving from the traditional adversary position to a "no fault" divorce. It is too early to tell how this easing of divorce will affect children. Just because we are able to do away with the question of who is at fault in divorce does not mean that we have done away with the question of who gets custody of the children. This issue may be more difficult to resolve now than before.

Day-to-Day Care of Child(ren)

Whether the mother or the father gets custody of a child, trying to be both mother and father to that child is not an easy task. For one thing, the parent who stays is locked into the child's world more than the parent who is gone. In the best interest of the child and the parent, time needs to be provided for each to experience some solitude. Children as well as parents need some time to themselves—some time to think their own thoughts.

While being the parent who stays with the child can be confining, it can also be most rewarding. In our estimation, being a parent is the most important job you will ever have in life. Bernard M. Baruch said: "The housewife is the most important person. She holds the world together. Mothers are the most unselfish, the most responsible people in the world."[4] Fathers can also perform this nurturing, supportive role with children. Our purpose is not to say who is more important to the child. We do mean to say, though, that whether you are the mother or the father, you are one of the two most important people in the world to your child. No one else will ever have the opportunity to influence your child as much as you do.

Because of the tremendous influence that a parent does have on his child, the divorced parent who is providing a home for his child should keep several things in mind.

The child will need to be reminded from time to time, particularly at first, that he is in no way responsible for the strife, the separation, and divorce which followed.

Regardless of the feelings a parent has toward his former mate, the child must get the message that he is loved by both parents. Neither parent should use the child as a sounding board for personal bitterness.

The child in a one-parent home is faced with more responsibilities than children with two parents and should be given extra measure of understanding and encouragement.

The child of divorce has had to "leave mother and father" (emotionally) much sooner than a child from an intact family.

As a child grows and becomes more mature, he should be encouraged to make a life for himself apart from the conflicts of his parents.

Parents should not put the child in the position of being a spy or a tattletale, thereby prolonging their fighting at the expense of the child.

Playing One Parent Against Another

When you recall your own childhood, you probably have little difficulty remembering times when you succeeded in playing one parent against another. It may have been a situation in which you (as the child) wanted your parents to buy you a toy or some other item. Not having succeeded with one parent, you went to the other and presented just the right amount and right kind of information to get a favorable response.

Or you may have wanted permission to go someplace or do something with friends. Again, calling upon your knowledge and previous experience, you went first to the parent who was most likely to grant your wish.

This happens with all children to some extent, not just children of divorce. Children whose parents are divorced, though, may use this particular technique to meet some of their special needs. If a child feels that his parents do not like him, he may say bad things about the absent parent when he is in the presence of the other, to get that parent to like him more. We have already discussed the fact that parents sometimes encourage this behavior as a means of continuing to fight with one another. In the first instance the child is put in the middle, unfairly. In the latter situation, the child is attempting to put the parent in the middle to meet his own emotional needs. Neither situation is desirable. If the child, on his own, is attempting to belittle the other parent, the parent who is with him needs to offer assurance that he is loved and accepted. If the reality of the situation is that one of the parents does not like the child, nothing is gained by the other parent's trying to convince him otherwise. On the other hand, it does not help the child to encourage his speaking critically of the absent parent.

Another way children of divorce may play one parent against another is to take advantage of the situation to get things from them that they really do not need. For instance, the child may make up stories to tell each parent that cause that parent to bestow special favors upon him in order to be spiteful to the other parent. Parents need to be aware of this kind of manipulation and take measures to stop it.

Lack of Order

In order to feel secure, each of us needs a certain amount of predictability in life. This need is greater for children than adults. And among children, predictability is needed most by children who have experienced disruptions such as divorce.

Before a separation or divorce actually takes place, many children hear threats of separation or divorce. Anger and arguing have likely been a part of many conversations. The child can identify with these emotions since he, too, is experiencing frustration and anger. Threats of leaving, though, are harder for a child to accept.

Equally as difficult for the child is to have one parent angrily walk out for a temporary period and then return unexpectedly. In some cases, this same experience may be repeated weeks or months later. Why is the latter situation more difficult for the child to deal with than anger and arguing? There are at least two reasons. We have already alluded to the first: children can readily identify with feelings of frustration and the anger and may express these feelings in ways similar to the parents. A more important reason, though, is one that we have learned from people who have spent a lifetime observing and studying children. They tell us that it is not uncommon for children to have a strong unconscious fear of being deserted and abandoned by one or both parents. For a child to live in the constant threat of a parent's leaving may be worse than having it actually happen. Assuming that one parent is gone, what are some ways the remaining parent can restore some predictability in the life of a child?

Daily Schedule

One way to help a child feel more secure is to institute a routine which the child can count on from day to day. Getting-up time, study time, time with parent, and time to be alone are examples of some activities which should take place at about the same time each day. Establishing this kind of routine is not only good for the child, it is also quite beneficial to the parent. Why do we offer a suggestion which seems so simple and self-evident? We take the time to discuss this because of the large number of families we have seen in which simple routines are lacking. This is a problem not only for single-parent families but also for families with both parents present.

It seems to us that one of the routines which should be emphasized is mealtime. Many adults can recall pleasant childhood memories of mealtime. Throughout history, mealtime has been important to families. The Bible has much to say about mealtime experiences and the lessons to be learned from them. If a family moves away from predictable times when all of the members of the household share a meal together, one can predict with some degree of accuracy that something of the family's togetherness is lost. The shift may happen so gradually that the members of the family are not even aware that it is happening. It can happen as easily in a two-parent family as a single-parent family. If families do not insist on having at least one meal together each day, when is there time for conversation, for sharing experiences, for discussing problems encountered during the day, for sharing moments of joy and triumph, for learning from one another—for being a family? When is there time?

Traditionally, Jewish and Chinese families have emphasized the importance of mealtime. In practice they have insisted that all members of the family be present when the meal is served. It seems more than a coincidence to us that there has also been a tradition of little or no juvenile delinquency among Jewish and Chinese families. The records will show that among Jewish and Chinese families in which this mealtime practice has diminished, problems with the children have increased. We strongly recommend the importance and security of schedules, routines, and rituals, especially regarding mealtime.

It is interesting that one of the most winsome and moving invitations to salvation in the Bible likens it to eating a satisfying meal. "Behold, I stand at the door, and knock: if any man hear my voice, and open the door, I will come in to him, and will sup with him, and he with me" (Rev. 3:20).

Outside Activities

The parent who stays not only has the greater responsibility for establishing and maintaining normal routines within the home, but he or she also has the primary responsibility for helping the child relate to others outside the home in a meaningful way. We are thinking of such things as school, church, scouts, sports, clubs, music lessons, and other outside interests. We are not implying that a child should be involved in all of these things. The interests and talents of the child will determine the extent to which a child can participate productively in activities outside the home. The parent who is not at home may offer some assistance here. However, the truth of the adage "If it is to be, it is up to me" applies primarily to the parent who stays.

Whether you are the mother or the father, if you are primarily responsible for the care of the children, your child needs your physical presence as well as time away from you. This is true for boys and girls, particularly adolescent children. As children become older, they need to break the ties of dependence on mother and dad. A child does not get to be a responsible adult simply by getting bigger. He has to leave behind something of what he was and replace it with something else. This fact applies to relationships as well as to tangible things. It is a difficult task for parents to allow children to grow in this way. Few of us truly wish to see our child break free of the bonds of our love and become this outsider who has his own ambitions, dreams, and thoughts—some of which may be quite unlike our own.

It is not easy for most mothers and fathers to let go of their children as they get older. The temptation to hold the child close to you—too close—may be even greater if you are the parent who has the primary responsibility for rearing the child. How can a parent know if he/she is doing this kind of holding? How can one determine the balance between parental love which communicates appropriate restraint and caring, and the necessity for allowing the child the freedom to become independent of one's constant guidance?

There are no easy answers. Someone once said, "For every difficult and complex question there is a simple answer—and it is always wrong." This seems to be the case as parents try to determine how to relate to their children. A good starting place, however, is simply to accept the fact that *a child is a child*. He is at the beginning of his journey as a human being with much to learn and a long way to go. Many things are involved in being a child, and we will all be helped by keeping some of them in mind.

A child is—

A product of slow and gradual growth.

Able to sit before he can stand.

Selfish before he is altruistic.

Dependent on others before he can depend on self.

Able to babble before he is able to talk.

Able to say no before he can say yes.

Subject to the laws of growth in all of his abilities.

What this means for us as parents is that we must take a child where he is and help him move to the next stage of development with a minimum of misunderstanding and unnecessary conflict. We give the child freedom to make choices and assume increasing responsibilities as he is able to demonstrate his ability to handle this freedom. This freeing is done in scores of small ways from day to day. When it becomes apparent that the child is unable to handle the responsibility, the parent simply takes it back. So, you see, there is a constant give and take in this whole maturing process. The parent should not expect the child to learn from a few words of instruction what it has taken him/her twenty or thirty years to learn by process of painful experience and discovery.

We emphasize that the stages of development cannot be rushed or hurried. A child must be allowed to progress at his own pace. A child should not be pushed faster than he is capable of going, neither should he be held back when he is able to move in the direction of responsible independence.

Problems of the Parent Who Goes

As the parent who leaves, you may have the feeling that it is too late to change things. The parent who leaves may reason that the marriage has failed and that the time for making any positive contribution to the family is forever gone. While it may be true that you as husband or wife have not made a success of your marriage, it does not follow that you must fail in your role as parent. Divorce severs the relationship of husband and wife, but it does not sever your relationship as parent of your child. Regardless of what happens to you as a husband or wife, you will always be the father or mother of your children.

All is not lost. Much remains to be done. Your children need you now more than ever. In fact, you may find that you will order your priorities in such a way that the children will now have first claim on some of your quality time. Only you can decide the extent and significance of your relationship with your children. They will have more choices as adults, but the way you relate to them while they are children will determine, to a large extent, how they will relate to you as an adult. It is still within your power to help your children develop into the kind of persons you wish them to be.

Time with Children

The primary resource at your disposal as you attempt to help your children is *time*. To be sure, there is a continuing need for financial assistance. This support may be legally required. Even if you were not required to provide financial assistance, you would likely choose to do this anyway in the best interest of your children.

Providing money for your children may be one of the easiest things you can do. Providing time in your schedule when you can be with them may be more difficult. One reason for this is that today's theme often appears to be "Do your own thing." Most of us who are parents of young children haven't experienced a great depression or a global war. In our own period of growing up, we were not required to make the kinds of sacrifices made by previous generations of parents. We are accustomed to modern conveniences and liberalized standards of behavior. These factors may have contributed to a more self-indulgent attitude on the part of all of us. Children, however, still require *commitment* and *sacrifice*. It doesn't hurt us to give up a night out occasionally or a Saturday afternoon football game or a pleasure trip or a number of other things that occupy a great deal of our time.

In some families the husband and wife argue over who should provide what benefits for the children. Urie Bronfenbrenner, an authority on child development, has aptly put it, "Please God, let it be someone!"

We cannot emphasize too strongly how important time is to the child. The sad fact is, however, that after the divorce the parent who goes usually sees less and less of the children. Again, in most cases the parent who goes is the father. Repeatedly, we see children whose problems stem from having busy, successful fathers. These fathers are the ones who find virtually no time to give to their children unless something goes wrong. For instance, sometimes they are faced with conference after conference with school authorities because of problems their children are having. These are well-meaning fathers who might have prevented some of the problems had they recognized how important it is for a child to be important to his or her father.

If you want to have a more meaningful place in your child's life and want your child to feel pride, warmth, and love toward you, we offer these further suggestions regarding time:

Telephone your child while you are on a business trip.

During phone calls, spend time listening to your child and showing a sincere interest in what is going on while you are away.

Emphasize your wish to be with your child, in spite of the demands of your work.

If you have visiting privileges, try having lunch with your child at school.

When you spend time with your child, don't make him feel guilty that you have given up more important things.

Allow your child to eat lunch with you occasionally, meet your colleagues, shake hands with them, and participate in conversation.

Of course, birthdays and other special events must not be forgotten.

Children communicate by whatever means are available to them. One way they have of telling you they need you is to get into trouble. Do not wait until your child has gone to this extreme in pleading for more of your time and interest. Arrange your responsibilities in such a way that your child feels as important as anything else that claims your commitments.

Kenneth N. Taylor, father of ten children, and the man who did the "paraphrase-translation" of *The Living Bible*, was asked what he would do differently if he had the opportunity to do over again the things he had done in the last thirty years. His reply: "I would spend more quality time with my children, I would pay more attention to showing my wife that I appreciate her, and I would examine myself more thoroughly to detect spiritual faults and have them dealt with by my Lord much earlier in the personal spiritual process."[5]

I suppose Kenneth Taylor has voiced the sentiments of us all, married or divorced. If we are honest with ourselves, most of us would agree that we could have and should have spent more quality time with our family. We can't change the past, however. No matter how much we wish it were different, it remains as it was lived and experienced. Only its consequences creep over into the present.

Aldous Huxley opened the foreword to a later edition of the 1932 classic, *Brave New World*, by observing : "Chronic remorse, as all the moralists are agreed, is a most undesirable sentiment. If you have behaved badly, repent, make what amends you can and address yourself to the task of behaving better next time."

What Huxley seems to be saying is that we should not be chained to our past failures but always be willing to make a new start. It is never too late to spend more time with your children. As our children get older, though, there is less opportunity to spend meaningful time with them. For one thing, they develop interests of their own and do not want or need us as much as when they were younger.

Temptation to Overindulge Children

A real temptation for the parent who is not living with the child is to overindulge him. By overindulgence we mean the giving of unneeded material things as a way of trying to make up for one's physical absence. You may be thinking, "But this happens in many homes where parents are not divorced." And you are quite right. But overindulgence is never correct or desirable.

If you find yourself falling into this trap, ask why and whether or not what you are doing is in the best interest of the child. (You may observe throughout this book that we repeat the phrase "the best interest of the child." If we seem to be emphasizing this concept, we mean to.) Overindulgence may be coupled with a failure to punish or discipline the child. The end result of this failure may mean that the child will have more difficulty getting along with the parent with whom he lives.

Limiting gifts to special occasions will help a child enjoy them more and will encourage a child to do and make more things on his own. Spend more time talking about matters which really bring parents closer to their children. Discuss personal things like worries and problems. Talk with them truthfully and honestly about what both of you feel and think about many subjects. Instead of a constant giving of gifts, time together should be a sharing of hopes, disappointments, experiences, and plans. Finally, make those precious moments together times for listening to each other's ideas.

Child-Rearing Responsibilities

The parent who has been given the custody of a child obviously has the greater child-rearing responsibilities. He or she is with the child on a daily basis and must be prepared to offer the continual guidance that a child needs. The importance of the task was summarized by the American statesman John Hay. He said that saving a little child and bringing him to his own is a much better business than loafing around the throne. We agree with the statement. Being a king or the President of the United States is no more important a job than being a good parent. If we view parenthood in this way, we are going to feel a need for divine guidance in our roles as parents.

Harry Truman, who was President and parent, was once asked

how a parent should advise his children. He is reported to have said, "I have found the best way to give advice to your children is to find out what they want and then advise them to do it." We all wish it were that simple. For complex problems there are no simple solutions. Helping children grow to mature, responsible adults is not simple or easy.

"What does all of this have to do with me if I am not staying with the child?" one might ask. For an answer let's look at one of the oldest questions in history: "Am I my brother's keeper?" (Gen. 4:9*b*). Well, technically, probably most of us would agree that Cain was not his brother's keeper. That is, he may not have had legal responsibility for the welfare of his brother. He had a responsibility, though, that was greater than legal responsibility. While Cain may not have been his brother's keeper, *he was his brother's brother*, with all that is involved in being a brother. One may not, in the strict legal sense, be his child's daily keeper, but he is his child's parent, with all that is involved in being a parent.

Each year at Harvard University this Baccalaureate Hymn, written by William Tans'ur, is sung at graduation time:

> Let children learn the mighty deeds
> Which God performed of old,
> Which, in our younger years, we saw,
> And which our fathers told,
> Our lips shall tell them to our sons,
> And they again to theirs,—
> That generations yet unborn
> May teach them to their heirs.

These lines seem to be based on a song written some one thousand years before the birth of Christ. That song, in part, states:

> I will open my mouth in a parable: I will utter dark sayings of old: Which we have heard and known, and our fathers have told us. We will not hide them from their children, shewing to the generation to come the praises of the Lord, and his strength, and his wonderful works that he hath done. . . . That the generation to come might know them, even the children which should be born; who should arise and declare them to their children (Ps. 78:2-4,6).

Our Judeo-Christian heritage places a great emphasis on the importance of children. We need to become concerned when we see evidence that our nation is about to decide that it is not important to be a good parent. You may not be present, but you are still a parent. Be the best one possible.

Suggestions for Both Parents

Always Relate

An idea basic to the whole ecology movement is that everything in the universe is related to everything else. The complex world in which we live is continually demonstrating this truth. What happens to children—our own and others—eventually affects all of us. I think this is one thing Nicholas Hobbs had in mind when he said, "In the thinness of community, restoration of a common commitment to children becomes increasingly urgent. If I neglect my child, your child will pay for my neglect ten times over. If a child goes to bed hungry, we are all diminished by this distress. When a rat bites a child at night, it bites all children. And you and I are responsible."[6]

Whether you are the parent who stays or the parent who goes, you will always have a responsibility for your child. True, the parent who is with the child on a day-to-day basis is faced with the most immediate need, but both are parents. The child has a right to a continued relationship with the parent who is away, and both parents have the responsibility to see that the child is not deprived of this. In the best interest of the child, which, as we have said, should always be the first concern of parents, mutual cooperation can assure the child's right to continued access to both parents.

Always Concerned

Though parents may live in different households, be separated by many miles, develop talents and interests that are quite different, yet they are still related in one significant way. To their children they will always be mother and father. Because this is true—

Be consistent (with yourself and one another)
Be in agreement on significant matters
Be interested in your child's activities

Be your child's parent, with all that is involved in being a parent.

What Does All This Mean for Me?

This chapter can mean as little or as much as you want it to mean. It is written with both parents in mind; specific suggestions are offered for each. Whether you are the parent who is still with the child or the one who has gone, you will find suggestions that will be of continuing help in the section of the chapter, "Problems Common to Both." Of course, the other section which applies specifically to you is written with your needs in mind. It contains information which other people, like yourself, have found to be helpful. Reading this section carefully should help you profit from the experience of others, as well as put your own experience into proper perspective.

In human relationships, we are often successful in proportion to our ability to put ourselves in the other person's place—to see things from the other person's point of view. Your ability to do this may be sharpened if you will read the section addressed to the other parent.

Andy's conversation with Timothy Nobles, the neighborhood grandfather, centered on Andy's hope of getting into a special training program sponsored by a local union.

"What are their requirements?" Mr. Nobles asked, interrupting the glowing picture Andy was painting.

"Requirements?" Andy asked blankly.

"Yes. Do you have to have a certain level of education? Like your high school diploma?"

"Oh, that. Well, you have to be a graduate."

"And?" Mr. Nobles's question was understood.

"I'm going to get down the next few months and finish my work. I really am, you know."

"That's good, Andy," Mr. Nobles replied. Then he talked directly to Andy about the self-discipline such study would take.

Andy commented: "I guess I've never had much discipline. Now my granddad, boy, sometimes he really got on me if I didn't do right. But at school they never did make me do anything, not as good as I could."

As Andy talked on, Mr. Nobles kept thinking how accurate this insight was.

"I guess you've needed more help than you've had so far in developing good self-discipline," Mr. Nobles commented aloud.

"Yeh, I guess so. After Mom and Dad got a divorce, she had to work, you know. She'd always come home too tired to put up with me if I was determined to have my own way."

"Andy, was there anyone else who helped you in those earlier years? I mean besides your grandfather."

"Oh, I had an uncle and an aunt. They don't live here. But my uncle used to write me cards and letters from all over the country when he traveled. One time in Sunday School when we all had to make a Father's Day gift, I sent him what I made."

If their conversation had a label it would probably read

3.
Significant Others

That title also describes the subject of this chapter. We will be dealing with the importance of some persons outside a child's immediate family as their lives and his entwine. These persons are potentially a tremendous resource for helping the child of divorce cope adequately with the problems he encounters.

With appreciation we recall those friends and relatives who early helped us see ourselves as persons of worth. Many of them probably did not realize that they were truly "significant others" to us. Their love and support was freely and naturally expressed in words, actions, and prayers. This chapter is dedicated to them and to the many men and women and boys and girls whose lives today are bringing richness and joy to many children, but particularly to the children of divorce.

As you study the chapter, you should develop an awareness of the potential of persons in the extended family, school, church, and community as helpers for the child of divorce. You will also learn how to tap these resources. At the conclusion of the chapter, you should be able to make at least tentative plans for involving such persons in helping one or more children of divorce for whom you are concerned.

Before we think more closely about different categories of people from which significant others are likely to come, let's consider what significant others can mean to the life of a child.

Significant others help shape a child's self-image. Even though there is the risk that they will damage a child's self-image, they are far more likely to improve that image.

Significant others help shape a child's values. Not only can they do so, they are sure to do so. Parents are not the sole influence in determining the values a child accepts and lives by.

Significant others provide emotional support to children. The child of divorce has already suffered a reduction in emotional support. Others, such as the people we will be talking about, can help fill that need.

Significant others can provide some experiences the divorced parent may not be able to provide because of his working hours and increased home responsibility. Significant others may, for instance, take children on shopping expeditions, to view historical sites, and to visit museums.

Significant others can also release some hours for the divorced parent to have for his personal growth and development.

Extended Family

Everybody talks about the extended family, but few of us live in one. Check your own family situation and that of your neighbors. How many houses on your block or units in your apartment complex shelter more than two generations? How many children do you know whose grandparents live in another town? How many have aunts or uncles or cousins who go to the same church they do?

Nevertheless, relatives form a significant group in the lives of children even in a mobile society. Being part of a large family—grandparents, aunts, uncles, cousins—is important to a child.

Each of these persons bears a distinctive relationship to the child. The dimension of the relationship is determined to some extent by society's expectations. Grandparents, according to folklore, are wise people who do kind things for young children. Grandmothers bake cookies and kiss away hurts. Grandfathers take walks with children and tell them entrancing stories of the long ago. Cousins are buddies and sometimes bullies.

The more significant aspects of these relationships are determined by the personal traits and attitudes of the persons involved. Some adults in the extended family simply don't care for children. Others relate easily to children. Some like children but treat them as objects, not as persons. Some children like their cousins; some do not.

Let's look at some attitudes which others in the extended family may have toward the child of divorce.

How Do They Feel?

Sometimes extended family members, even grandparents, resent a child. Perhaps they were never in favor of the marriage which brought the child into being. They may feel that the parent(s) tries to unload on them the major responsibility for caring for the child. Cousins may be jealous of the child if they feel he gets more than his rightful share of family attention.

Sometimes extended-family adults, even if they harbor no resentment, feel inadequate for the responsibility they perceive as theirs. These feelings are not the exclusive property of spinster aunts and bachelor uncles. Such misgiving may linger even in the heart of a relative who is doing a good job of rearing his own children.

In some cases the other adult members of a family feel guilty about the divorce which has taken place. Like the child who feels guilty because of his parent's divorce, an adult who never accepted a son-in-law or a brother-in-law or a niece by marriage may feel vaguely responsible. Such a sense of guilt is not the best of foundations for a good relationship with the child of divorce.

Other family adults may feel overly sentimental about the child of divorce. They may relate to him as a "poor little thing." This attitude can lead to a superficial relationship in which the child is seen, not as a whole person, but as an object of charity.

The attitudes we have talked about so far are all negative. But most adult relatives probably relate to the children in the wider family in terms of active love. They may not always have the insights which would be most helpful in the relationship. They may be far from expert in child rearing. Still they do surround the child with tender concern.

It would be a mistake to assume that any one adult has only one of the attitudes we have discussed. Even though one of these attitudes is dominant, the others may be present from time to time. And a variety of these attitudes can coexist.

What Can Be Expected of Them?

Before we try to deal more extensively with this question, remember that we must talk in generalities. When one thinks of a particular parent and a particular family member and a particular child, general observations are often inadequate.

The divorced parent cannot expect indulgence—either for himself or for his child. Even though other family members may have contributed to the breakup of a marriage, the responsibility rests squarely upon the divorcing parties. Other family members are under no obligation to act as if the divorced relative is a victim of circumstance, unfairly treated by a cruel and thoughtless ex-mate and by the world in general.

The divorced parent cannot expect other adults in the family to assume responsibility which is his. For instance, discipline of a child—its content and its methodology—remain the responsibility of the parent as long as he or she is mentally competent and emotionally stable enough to function adequately. This responsibility can never be tossed to others.

Nor can a divorced parent expect others to assume financial responsibility for him or her and the child. Divorce frequently brings a reduced standard of living. Two may be able to live as cheaply as one—but not when they live under separate roofs. Making up for the financial strain created by divorce is not the automatic responsibility of others.

What can a divorced parent legitimately expect from extended-family members? He should be able to expect love and emotional support as long as he does not demand that others condone his actions. The divorced parent should expect the normal sort of helping-out which his family members customarily provide one another. This help probably includes child-sitting from time to time and inclusion in family events such as birthday celebrations.

This list of what a divorced parent should and should not expect of his parents and of his brothers and sisters and in-laws emphasizes an important truth. The divorced parent is, in spite of the strength of the extended family, still responsible for himself and for his child in every way which truly matters.

How Can Parents and the Extended Family Work Together?

Evaluate these suggestions in the light of your own experiences.

Family adults who genuinely care about one another must find ways to acknowledge openly and calmly their feelings about situations which confront them. The grandparent who feels that too much is being thrust upon him should be allowed to say so. The parent who feels that he is not being adequately supported emotionally should be allowed to say so.

Family adults who share responsibility for a child must agree upon ground rules. And then they must stick by the rules until those rules are altered by mutual consent. For instance, basic approaches to discipline must be worked out. If a certain act is to be considered against the rules, then it is against the rules regardless of who is present when it is performed. If a certain act rates a certain punishment, then that act rates that punishment regardless of who must administer the discipline in a certain situation.

The ground rules may include free time for the parent and for the grandparent, if he or she serves as caretaker on a regular basis. Each party involved should protect this free time.

Family adults who are genuinely concerned for one another respect each person's distinctiveness. While ground rules are agreed upon and rigorously adhered to, each adult still remains himself. In most instances these differences enrich the life of the total family unit.

Family adults who are genuinely concerned for the welfare of a child stick to their responsibilities. The child of divorce may already feel that he has been abandoned by a person of great importance in his life. If members of the extended family play at being supportive and then withdraw that support when the going gets rough, they perpetrate another equally disastrous desertion.

School and Day-Care and Steady Sitters

Not every child of divorce has immediate access to an extended family. But nearly every child of divorce is in a nursery school, a kindergarten, or an elementary school. If not, he likely is in a day-care center or has a regular sitter or a number of less-than-regular sitters.

Who are these people? What are they like? How do they influence the child? What kind of people ought they to be? How does a parent relate effectively to these persons? You are probably bubbling with other questions. Let's see if we can answer at least a few of your questions.

Some of those regular sitters and some of the less-than-regular sitters we have already talked about. They are members of the extended family. So let's spend this section of the chapter talking about sitters who are not related to the family.

One working mother found another mother in her neighborhood who was willing to look after her preschooler. This arrangement was convenient for both the mothers involved. The stay-home caretaker had no special qualifications beyond her willingness. In time the working mother reached the conclusion that family standards in that home were not consistent with the standards she wanted to maintain. The arrangement was terminated.

Another working mother checked the classified ads in the local shopping news. She found several persons who were looking for one or two children to keep in their homes during the day. By visiting three of these women, she found a home in which she felt her children would be well cared for.

A divorced father ran an ad in the newspaper for a housekeeper who would help with his children. From the several responses he received, he selected two he was willing to try. In view of the transportation problems which one of the two had, he finally chose the one he initially had considered less qualified.

None of these sitters was a professional in the field of child care. This fact alone does not mean that these persons were not good caretakers. After all, most parents are certainly not professionals. In fact, most parents feel a lot like one grandfather who attended a seminar on young children. He later commented to his son, "If your mother and I had known when you and your brother were small what we learned in that seminar, we wouldn't have had the courage to raise you."

Another sizable group of children of divorce are cared for in nursery schools or day-care centers of one sort or another. Many of these schools and centers are church-operated. Some are community agencies with enrollment limited to children of low-income parents.

Day-care institutions are generally regulated by city, county, and/or state agencies. The requirements vary from place to place, and the rigidity of enforcement may also vary. Still these legal rules do afford patrons some measure of assurance. Of course, a parent must still determine for himself whether or not the person to whom he entrusts his child is worthy of that trust.

Many children of divorce spend most of their days in public or private school. Some private schools provide child care after regular school hours. Few public schools provide such an on-premises service. Many children in public schools split their away-from-home hours between the classroom and a child-care institution or the home of a sitter.

A child of school age spends much of his school-year day in the company of a professional: his classroom teacher. The primary responsibility of this teacher is, of course, to help the child learn what our society expects every competent adult to know. At the same time, the teacher's education and experience are designed to provide him with insights which enable him to support children in nonacademic crises. The majority of classroom teachers live up to their responsibility as caretakers.

But there is yet another group of significant others involved in the settings we are talking about. You are right: A child's peers are significant others. And their significance increases as the child grows older.

Not a lot can be done about the brothers and sisters with whom a child must grow up. They, too, belong to the family. They, too, are subject to the stresses and strains the rest of the family endures.

Not a lot can be done about the classmates which a child encounters once his formal education begins. A parent can't just decide that his child's classmates are unsuitable and place his child in another class where all the classmates are suitable. Nor can he demand that all other children change their ways. Helping a child cope with children of diverse backgrounds and standards is an integral part of child rearing.

In some other settings, parents can regulate the exposure of their children to peers they feel are not suitable. Such regulation can be done before a child is entrusted to a neighbor or to a center by discussing with the caretaker what matters most to the parent. Regulation can also be achieved by withdrawing a child from an undesirable setting. Even so, a parent must decide whether it is better to remove the child from the setting or to help him cope with it.

How Do They Feel?

The range of feelings toward divorced parents and their children is as wide among teachers and caretakers as is the range in the general population. Because of personal experiences and rearing, some of these persons take a dim view of divorced persons and have a bedrock conviction that any marriage can be made to work if only the parties are willing to do so. Because of personal experiences and rearing, other persons in the group have special sympathy for the divorced person and for his children. Others are simply indifferent.

Few such persons let their attitude toward divorce in general significantly affect the way they treat a particular child. Certainly the people who work with children—the people we are considering—are prochild. If any of the caretakers ever mistreats a child, his actions are not likely to be rooted in the marital status of the child's parents.

What Can Be Expected of These Helpers?

We've talked already about what a divorced parent may expect from the extended family. He can expect some of the same things from caretakers and peers involved in the day-to-day life of his child—some things, but not exactly the same things.

At the top of the list of what he cannot legitimately expect is indulgence. If you read chapter 1 carefully, you faced a basic fact in American life: Divorce is common. Those who associate with divorced persons and with their children can make some limited concessions for a limited period of time. But to let the fact of divorce dominate every relationship is unworkable and unwise.

Another negative: The divorced parent cannot expect caretakers, teachers, and peers to inculcate the moral values the parent has. Classroom teachers are likely to support standard American virtues such as honesty and patriotism and fair play. But they are not charged with the responsibility of influencing each child to adopt the moral standards of his parents. They are not, for instance, likely to help a child develop the parental attitude toward sex, liquor, drugs, and things such as abortion.

Fortunately, there are some pluses in the picture. The divorced parent can expect these teachers and other caretakers to accept his child. These significant others must be able to love with concern and compassion. They may demand a great deal of a child because of their own high standards as well as their realization of the child's true potential. But even if the child does not live up to expectation, caretakers and teachers can still be expected to accept him.

Another plus which the divorced parent is entitled to expect is professional ethics. Even the caretaker who is not by training a professional should be careful to protect the family secrets which he discovers in dealing with a child. Persons who truly love children are usually willing to put the welfare of the families they deal with above the pleasure of a tongue that wags at both ends.

How Can Parents, Teachers, and Caretakers Work Together?

As in the case of the extended family, a few rules are in order.
Parents must be fair about what they expect from the caretakers

and teachers. None is perfect. Each has limitations.

Parents must be honest about what they want from the caretaker or teacher. Without being demanding, a parent can tell the others what he hopes they will do and will mean in his child's life. In open discussion parents and others can come to share goals.

Parents can live up to their end of bargains struck with teachers or caretakers. Sometimes a "bargain" is not easy to keep. For instance, when a child is eager to play, a parent may wish he didn't have to call time out for homework. But he must. A person keeping a child in his home knows what time a parent gets off work and has, unless special arrangement is made, contracted to care for the child only until the parent can arrive. To leave the child on and on without notice is unfair.

Parents and caretakers or teachers must establish clearly understood ground rules. Some ground rules are set by boards of education rather than by classroom teachers. A parent is generally better off accepting these rules with a minimum of complaint. Ground rules include items such as schedules, rate of pay, and time of payment in the case of caretakers.

Evaluation of the relationship is in order from time to time. Parent-teacher conferences, for instance, are as much tools for parents as for teachers.

People at Church

Another source of significant others in the life of a child—any child—is the church. Unfortunately not every child of divorce is involved in the life of a local community of believers.

Those persons in the church family who are most likely to become significant to a child are those with whom the child has the closest association. These "first-line" people are the adults who teach or lead him in the organization of the church. The children who participate with him in these organizations are also likely to become important people to him.

If you were a churchgoer in the early years of your life, recall the adults who taught you in Sunday School and other church organizations. You will likely be able to call by name three or four persons who profoundly influenced your life. As you think about these people, compare the amount of time you actually spent with them to the amount of time you spent with your parents or schoolteachers. The time you shared with adults at church was probably only a fraction of the time you shared with others. Yet these church people were truly significant to you.

Sunday School teachers or other church organization leaders may spend only an hour a week with a child, plus a few social times a year and a few visits and telephone calls during a year. Yet they are quite likely to become significant persons in the child's life.

Another group of church workers who are potentially significant persons in the life of a child are those who work with, teach, and recreate with the child's parents. The involvement of these persons with a child is usually indirect, but the child may, nonetheless, feel their concern for him. He may so enjoy being accepted by them that their influence is out of proportion to the time they spend with him.

One step removed, in most instances, from the men and women who work directly with a child and his parent is the professional church staff. In many congregations, the entire professional staff is composed of one person: the pastor. In other situations, several persons may be full-time employees of the church with special training for the ministries they perform. Your church may have a music director, a minister of Christian education, and one or more ministers who have responsibility for work with an age group.

These persons are, or can be, significant others in the life of a child and his parent. Church staff members are nearly always caring people who are ready to give any help possible. Many times they are highly qualified, both by experience and training, to provide guidance and counseling in crises, big and little.

How Do They Feel?

All of these people—the child's peers, the adult's peers, the men and women who teach or lead in church organizations, and the professional church staff—are individuals. Each of them brings unique feelings to every experience. It is only fair for us to consider some feelings which these persons are likely to have toward a divorced person and his or her child.

The most prevalent feeling is likely to be sympathy. Few dedicated Christians are hardhearted. On the contrary, church people generally feel intensely the hurt of others. Feeling this hurt, they are usually warm and tender in their regard for and treatment of any person who has been hurt.

Being sympathetic with a person's difficult situation, however, is not the same as condoning all that the person does. One of the challenges faced by the Christian community is how to provide support for the person who divorces while still holding high the standard of a lifelong commitment as the basis of marriage. The tension created in individuals by this challenge frequently leads to mixed feelings about the divorced person. While entirely sympathetic with the problems which the divorced person experiences, the church worker may feel that this misery is self-induced. He may wish to include the divorced person in his circle of friends while wondering how his own child will evaluate the situation.

A father talked to his daughter about the divorce which was under way in another family. The girl, sensing her father's tension, said: "Well, it is their own business. If they want to get a divorce, I don't think that is any concern of ours."

"Oh, yes, it is" her dad quickly replied. "When they married they took public vows and made some promises to God and to all of us. Their divorce is a concern of mine because it seems to be teaching you that divorce is OK." Because he liked the two people involved in the divorce and was distressed by their difficulties, this man had mixed feelings about his and his children's relationship to them.

One need not—probably should not—expect all Christians to be open and loving toward all divorced persons. Some may be so concerned about maintaining the sanctity of the home that they overreact to divorce. Some church people have themselves been deeply hurt by divorce—the divorce of their parents, their own divorce, the divorce of their children, or a divorce among close friends. They may withdraw from contact with other persons in this sort of distress. In such feelings they are not greatly different from others in the general society.

In other words, a divorced parent can expect varied reactions and feelings among the significant others within his church family. Although these feelings may range from critical to warmly supportive, they will tend to be tempered by both compassion and the desire to uphold the standard of lifetime commitment in marriage.

What Can Be Expected of Church Friends?

The most obvious answer to the question is that one can expect church leaders to teach Christian doctrine and to instill Christian values. No matter what church leaders do, parents are still the key figures in helping children develop values, but church workers can certainly reinforce what a family does. A parent is taking a chance if he expects church leaders to provide all the guidance his child receives in understanding the basic tenets of the church, but church leaders do help greatly at this point.

One can also expect church leaders to accept the child of divorce and his parents. This acceptance is rooted in the nature of God, although it may sometimes be narrowed by human limitations.

A divorced parent can also expect church leaders to help him understand his child's needs. Many parents have, for instance, gained significant insights through family and parent conferences.

How Can Church Leaders and Divorced Parents Work Together?

In essence, the guidelines for this relationship do not differ from the guidelines for parents who are not divorced.

To begin with, the divorced parent must be ready for his child to be exposed to teachings about the family which may make him critical of those who divorce. Such a critical attitude is not a new dimension. Many children of divorce hate the thought of divorce and are critical of their parents' failure to achieve a lasting and happy marriage. The parent himself may be uncomfortable in dealing with his church's stance on divorce. And he may have to face the matter with his child as the child studies units dealing with family life.

Again, openness is needed on both sides. Neither the parent nor the church friend should try to conceal real feelings, though the expression of these feelings should be done tactfully.

The divorced parent should guard against defensiveness, just as he or she should be careful to avoid taking offense at comments about divorce in general. A group of friends were sharing a meal together when the topic of conversation turned to divorce. A particularly nasty divorce was rehashed. Then some general comments about divorce were made as if those comments applied equally to all divorced persons. When one member of the group fell silent and soon excused himself from the table, the others suddenly realized that this man was himself divorced. By then it was too late to retract the statements they had exchanged. Yet none wanted to judge this man in particular as they seemed to judge divorced persons in general.

Later one of the friends talked to the man, expressing the hope that he had not been hurt or offended. "Well, it does hurt, of course, to hear those things said," was his response. "I know that none of you means to apply all you said to me. But I apply them to myself," he concluded.

The divorced parent must be willing to let members of his or her church family become significant in the life of the child. This fact means that the divorced parent will sometimes have to go a second mile in seeing that his or her child gets to go on retreats, attend camp, go to or have a party for the class, and engage in similar activities. Most of all, it means that the child must be encouraged to be present every time the group meets and to make whatever outside preparation is needed for that participation.

Community Friends

Let's turn now to one more category of people from which significant others may come: the community at large. Adults and children alike are in almost constant touch with a wide variety of persons in the community: shopkeepers, service station attendants, doctors and their associates, repairmen, garbage collectors, newsboys, neighbors, political units, leaders of special interest groups. The list goes on and on. We limit the list to a few major segments of the population, leaving you to think about others who may be especially significant to you.

Significant others, like charity, begin at home. Neighbors will in many cases become significant others for any child. In this process, a selective factor usually operates. One becomes involved more deeply in the lives of some neighbors than of others because one more easily relates to those persons. The reason may be shared interests in gardening, music, art, church, reading, or sports. The reason may be that the children in two households are especially compatible. Or two families may hold like values and have similar life-styles. Or the two households may face like circumstances: divorce, for instance.

In a sense, adult neighbors form a peer group. Something draws all of these adults into the same neighborhood. That something may be as simple as finances: This is one place that the families can afford to live, or these adults may have been drawn into a neighborhood because of proximity to schools or because of the type of housing available. So the ideas and opinions of neighbors are likely to matter to any individual who lives in the area.

But peer groups for adults and even for children extend beyond the neighborhood. We've already talked about peer groups within the church for both parent and child. And we have talked about the fact that classmates form a peer group for children. In addition, business associates form a peer group for the working adult. These associates may include fellow laborers, customers, and suppliers.

None of these peer groups from community life has official standing. They simply form and constantly reshape with the addition of new persons and the loss of others. There is, however, another group of significant others which has a sort of official standing. These are the people who serve as leaders in community organizations.

This group is composed of such people as Cub Scout, Brownie, Scout, Campfire Girls, and athletic team leaders. Because these people are key figures in the work of an organization important to the child, they become important to him. Athletic coaches are a good example. Nearly every parent has discovered that what coaches say, do, and expect strongly influences team members. If one is supposed to do thus-and-so according to Coach, one must do it—and do it the way he has been told.

Another group which fits in the category of significant others from the community is baby- or child-sitters. We have already considered the people who serve as regular caretakers in school and home when a parent must work. At this point, let's consider the people who are sitters on a less structured schedule. Most parents try to maintain a relationship with at least one such sitter who comes to know the child well. That quality of acquaintance makes the sitter important in the child's life.

How Do They Feel?

The answer is directly related to the number of persons who become significant in the life of the child. Each person brings a special set of feelings to the relationship. These unique sets of feelings range all the way across the spectrum. As much as the divorced person may think that these persons are concerned about his marital status, most of them are not particularly conscious of the situation one way or another. In the context of these relationships, the fact that one is divorced or never married or remarried or happily married to his one-and-only marriage partner is rarely the dominant factor.

What Can Be Expected from Community Friends?

While neighbors may become substitute family, other persons, such as Scout leaders, are not likely to become deeply involved with a family except at the point of contact: the child's activity in a particular group. This fact applies to all families regardless of the marital status of the parents. Of course, some of these relationships may flower into something more meaningful because of shared interests, common heritage, economic necessities, or other reasons. Even so, few persons from such groups are likely to become substitute parents for a child of divorce except in a limited way.

Again, let us remind you that divorced parents cannot expect community friends to make concessions to their children. A leader of a group may, of course, adjust schedules when possible to accommodate to the working parent's hours. But one cannot be expected to tolerate behavior one would correct in other children. A coach cannot be expected to make the key figure on the team a child of divorce who has less skill and potential than some child from a home which includes both parents.

How Can Parents and Community Friends Work Together?

To begin with, neither party should demand more than the relationship can comfortably yield. Having a coach who is also a good friend of the family may be great as far as a child is concerned. But coaches cannot be close friends with every family represented among the team members. If the coach is fair with the child and is competent as a coach, this is enough.

However, a parent, divorced or not, can gain a great deal from working closely with such persons as the need arises. If a child has problems of relationship with a leader or with group members, a parent can often talk the situation over with the leader. Together they can help the child and others handle the problem intelligently. Occasionally a child is lucky enough to be involved with persons of unusual insight into children. When this is the case, a parent may improve and expand his own understanding of his child through conversation with this person.

The parent can help make these relationships effective in his child's life by intelligent cooperation with the leaders of such groups. If the parent feels comfortable with what is demanded or requested of him, he should do his best to comply. The time for handling limitations, such as those created by the parent's work hours, is when the child joins an organization, rather than after he has become deeply involved in it.

Always the basic rules of neighborliness apply. Friends avoid imposing on each other. When one needs help he asks for it, clearly defining what he needs and expecting no more than the other party indicates he can deliver. Contracts, however informal, are made to be lived up to. Expressions of appreciation from time to time help.

Surrogates

One real need of families of divorce is persons who can help fill the gap left by the departure of one parent. The people we have so far discussed do help fill this gap in varying degrees. They can be considered surrogate parents or grandparents.

In the past society has usually recognized the need of a boy to have a man around the house. And a lot has been said about a girl needing a mother-figure to model after. Now we realize that boys also need mother-figures and girls need father-figures if they are to make successful adjustments. In the absence of one parent or the other, they need surrogates.

Being a surrogate parent or grandparent usually involves a closer relationship than merely being a good friend. If this closeness can be sustained, it has great potential for providing a wonderful kind of support for the child of divorce. But we need to consider answers to several key questions as we think about this sort of relationship.

What Are the Advantages of Such a Relationship?

Consider the relationship from three angles: that of the parent, that of the child, and that of the surrogate parent or grandparent.

The parent whose child has a surrogate parent stands to profit from the relationship. The child's dependence, physical and emotional, upon his stay-home parent is reduced. One more adult is involved in providing emotional support for the child. The concern which the parent feels for having deprived his child of a relationship with a model of the opposite sex can be relieved.

The child also stands to gain from such a relationship. Every child needs adult friends. One of the problems of our society is that adults and children are so frequently isolated from one another. The child's waking hours are filled with activities which throw him almost constantly into touch with children but allow little time with adults on an informal, unstructured basis.

The child of divorce particularly needs vital relationships with adults of the same sex as his absent parent. In these relationships he finds the models for his behavior which may be lacking in his home. A divorced mother said: "My daughter doesn't really know what it means to have a man around the place. My own parents divorced when I was a child, and now her father and I are divorced."

There are also advantages for the surrogate. Every adult needs some children as friends. Few experiences in life are more rewarding than those moments in which an adult is in close and happy communion with a child. There is even a satisfaction of sorts for the adult when he has to play the role of disciplinarian to a child he loves.

What Are the Pitfalls of Such a Relationship?

A surrogate relationship is subject to some of the same problems as real parenthood. For instance, the surrogate parent may lack the staying ability demanded for a sustained relationship. Or he may have values which at some points run counter to those of the parent, thus creating conflict in the heart and mind of the child.

Another pitfall which grabs some parents like a steel trap is jealousy. As much as most of us welcome the help of others in meeting the needs of our children, we turn green-eyed when these others become important to our children. It is not always easy to be told things about a child's inner life which he has freely shared with someone else. Nor does one always welcome being told that some other adult is the epitome of all that is good and interesting and fun.

How Does This Relationship Come into Being?

The answer is not clear-cut. But one thing is certain: The relationship cannot be forced. A church or a community group can appeal to the public or to church members for persons to play this role in the lives of motherless or fatherless children. And persons can respond to that challenge. But the forging of a genuine bond between a child and an adult requires more than a positive response to a challenge.

One can agree, for instance, to take a girl to a mother-daughter banquet or a father-daughter event. But whether one becomes a stand-in parent to the girl depends on a kind of chemistry between the willing adult and the child.

The implication of this fact is that a divorced parent is playing a risky game if he simply decides that a certain person would make a good stand-in parent for his or her child. He or she may request a family friend to do something like escort the child to some event. He may invite a family friend to go along on some family outing. But he cannot force the person to assume the role of surrogate parent or grandparent. Nor can he force his child to accept this kind of relationship with the person.

Can This Kind of Relationship Be Cultivated?

The answer to this question is, happily, yes. Once a parent feels that such a relationship is desirable, he or she can provide time for the adult and the child to be together. Without imposing upon the adult, the parent can include the adult in important family events: a long-planned outing, a birthday party. The parent can also help the child to appreciate the contribution which the adult makes to the family. While gratitude cannot be legislated, it can be nurtured. So a parent can help a child find ways to tell the adult that he is a treasured person: a sick card made by the child, a birthday celebration for the adult, a telephone call to share news of an important event in the child's life.

What Does This All Mean for Me?

In the introduction to the book, we suggested that all users read this chapter at one point or another. This means that we have tried to speak to all of the people who would be reading this book. You, of course, want help for you—not for people in general. So this section of the chapter is divided into several portions. It is fine for you to read all the portions, but you will want to deal most seriously with the section designed for people like you.

Divorced Parents

Begin to apply what you have discovered by listing the persons who are or who could easily become significant others in the life of your child. If necessary, check the headings of the chapter to remind you of categories from which these persons are likely to come.

Consider the relationship open to your child with at least one person from each of the categories. Then review the suggestions in the chapter sections which indicate how you can help make each relationship most meaningful. Mark the things you have done or can and will try to do.

Rewrite the things you can do in terms specifically applicable to the persons you have listed.

There you have the makings for a definite plan of action.

Extended Families, Teachers, Caretakers, Neighbors, and Community Leaders

Reread the section of the chapter which deals with persons like you.

List several children of divorce who are particularly important to you, children you would like to help.

Consider the suggestions which the section contains for making the adult-child relationship more meaningful and valuable to the child.

List some actions you can take in relationship to the child. Be sure to include what you might be able to do even if the parent is indifferent to the situation.

Church Staff Members

Consider your personal relationship to the children of divorce whose lives you touch. List some actions you can take to make these relationships most meaningful to the children.

Examine the needs of divorced parents who are a part of your congregation. When you reach chapter 6, keep these needs uppermost in your mind.

A person was heard to say on one occasion, "To do a good job, you must be sincerely interested in the product." Most people would agree with the self-evident wisdom of this axiom. What makes the statement more interesting, though, is to know that it was made by a young teacher.

One would hope that men and women are in the teaching profession because they are "sincerely interested in the product." All parents should also be interested in their children. Being interested in children and being skilled in dealing with them are not necessarily the same—for teachers or for parents. Everyone—parent, teacher, club leader, coach—who is concerned about children feels a need for help in this area from time to time. We are all concerned with

4.
Understanding
Children's
Behavior

What is behavior and how can one manage it? Behavior in its simplest form should be thought of as a verb rather than a noun. That is, behavior is active—it manifests itself in some kind of action. A person has behaved when he has made some response to his environment, which includes the people around him. A behavior is inappropriate, or maladaptive, when "It is a behavior that departs from the expectations and customs of the culture surrounding the individual marked as a deviator."[1] That is, his behavior is inappropriate (or misbehavior) when he responds in a way which is unacceptable to his family, friends, and society.

As you read this chapter you will discover some more about the meaning of behavior, and in chapter 5 a great deal more about how to manage it.

Thinking About Behavior

Where do we start if we are to improve behavior? If we wish our children to behave differently, we should first look at our own behavior. A truth worth underlining and reading again and again is this: The only authority one has over someone else's behavior is the control he has over his own behavior. The implications of this statement will be dealt with in some detail in this chapter. In chapter 5 you will discover that it is impossible to teach discipline if you are not disciplined. Also, likeness begets likeness—in behavior as well as heredity.

In chapters 4 and 5 we shall look at some of the common behavior problems of children and offer suggestions for dealing with them. Another important aspect of behavior we shall discuss is how we respond to children. How we communicate is of decisive importance; it affects a child's life for good or for bad. We are often not aware of whether our response to a child conveys acceptance or rejection. Yet how we respond to our children is of vital importance to them.

When children behave in ways that upset us, it is difficult to respond to them without becoming emotional ourselves. A child who is angry, jealous, self-centered, destructive, who has acquired bad language, or a number of other obnoxious behaviors, can upset us a great deal. This is understandable, for we do not want our children to behave this way. Obviously, the child needs to change. The behaviors which are causing difficulty for the child, for the parent, and for others need to be eliminated and new behaviors learned. This chapter will provide assistance in understanding troublesome behaviors, while chapter 5 will offer help in dealing with such behaviors.

As you read this chapter, you may discover that there are some aspects of your own behavior that you would like to change. You are in a better position to know this than anyone else. If you are not happy with yourself, then you can do something about your own behavior. Someone has said that the greatest achievement in life is the continual remaking of yourself so that you know how to live. Seven significant words you should remember as you read this chapter: *You can change if you want to.*

At the same time, we should remember that children of divorce need to be given special attention when they respond in positive and appropriate ways. It is so easy for all parents to fail to notice and give recognition to the things that children do well. It is precisely at these points of proper functioning that we need to tell the child what a good job he is doing and how proud we are of him. This is especially true of children of divorce who need a great deal of reassurance that they are loved and are persons of worth.

Five Important Ideas About Behavior

Behavior Is Caused

The first important idea that we can learn about behavior is that it is caused. When someone behaves in a negative, socially unacceptable way there is a reason for his behavior. Similarly, there is a reason for a person's behaving in a positive, growth-producing way. When we are confronted by some child's behavior which is difficult to understand, we should ask the questions:

What is the child trying to accomplish through his behavior? The adult needs to identify the goal which the child is trying to achieve.

Why did the child use this particular method? Again, we need to identify the ideas, skills, and so on which the child is using and how he happened to use these particular ones rather than others.

We should first look for a pattern of behavior in a child. When we see a pattern, before we try to interpret or judge it, we should ask the two aforementioned questions. Trying to answer these questions honestly and objectively will often give us the clue necessary for managing the behavior. There is considerable evidence that learning about the causes and consequences of behavior helps adults in their relationships with children. For instance, the child of divorce may attempt to convince the parent with whom he is living that he will do certain things or not do certain things if Mother and Dad will only get together again. In this instance what the child may actually be trying to do is to bring the parents together in the same household again. The goal he may be trying to achieve is not so much a reconciliation of the parents as a lessening of the guilt he may feel because he thinks he is responsible for the separation or divorce of his parents.

Behavior That Is Rewarded Continues

Most of us know that behaviors which are not rewarded are weakened and discontinue. Knowing this fact does not mean that we act upon it. In practice, we often reward the specific behavior that we would like to see discontinued. If a productive behavior in a situation is made more rewarding than a nonproductive behavior, the child will choose to behave in the manner which results in the greatest reward. For example, if a child is beginning to do failing work in school, this may be the child's way of getting the parent with whom he is living to pay more attention to him. The child may know that academic achievement is valued a great deal, and this is a sure way to get others to notice him/her, even though it may mean punishment.

In order that you do not misunderstand the meaning of the term, *reward* means much more than a tangible object. Approval, affection, attention, getting his name called, a wink, a nod—are all forms of reward. These rewards may be more important than any tangible gifts which could be given.

One final word about rewards: they always occur after the desired behavior, not before.

Expectation Brings Results

The best example we know of the positive results of expectation is a study conducted by Harvard psychologist Dr. Robert Rosenthal in cooperation with South San Francisco school principal Dr. Lenore Jacobson.[2] Their classic study sought to answer this all-important question: What do a teacher's expectations have to do with a pupil's achievement?

In a nutshell, some of the major findings of the study were these:
Expectations do affect learning.

If the teacher expects more, the child will achieve more.

Younger students were most affected by the teachers' expectations.

The findings of the study have tremendous implications for parents as well as teachers. The principle involved is called self-fulfilling prophecy—the idea that expecting a result can cause the result.

Actually, this notion is not a new one. It is part of folk wisdom that optimism will improve success in almost anything one does and that, conversely, pessimism will depress opportunities. It is almost equally accepted that our expectations of one another can exert similar influence. Goethe, the famed eighteenth-century German dramatist, wrote: "If you treat an individual as he is, he will stay as he is. But if you treat him as if he were what he ought to be, he will become what he ought to be and could be."

Behavior and Learning Are Always in the Present Tense

In trying to determine if something is behavior, apply the "Dead Man's Test" to it. That is, if a dead man can do it, it isn't behavior and should not be taught. For example, silence is not a behavior, so do not try to teach it. When you assign a child a dead position, he may act through it and you have lost the possibility of behavior occurring. One reason it is important to define behavior is that we need to make the distinction between behavior and words. You see, we often punish words and pay off behavior. For example, when a child admits to doing something wrong, the child may be punished immediately. If this happens repeatedly, it is not difficult to see how the child may conclude that telling the truth results in punishment. If this is the message which is being communicated, the child may be learning how to be dishonest. Therefore, reward and punishment should be tied more to actions than to words.

Learning is not only in the present tense, it is also personal. It is a constant interplay between the learner and his environment, the

teacher and the student, the parent and his child. George Bernard
Shaw had Eliza Doolittle explain that, the difference between a lady
and a flower girl is not how she behaves, but how she's treated.

Children Believe Their Parents

Children do believe their parents, and this can be a blessing or a
curse. It can be a blessing if the child gets the message that he is
loved, that he should love himself, that he is important, that he
should wonder and ask why, that his opinion and ideas are valued.
On the other hand, a child's believing his parents can be a curse if he
gets the message that he is no good, that he is stupid, that he can't do
anything right, that he is clumsy, or that he is like someone the parent
dislikes.

We now know that a child's first and most important teachers are
his parents. The significance of this statement is even more pronounced when we hear Jesse Stuart sum up his life's experience as a
teacher, school administrator, and poet by saying: "I am firm in my
belief that a teacher lives on and on through his students. Good
teaching is forever and the teacher is immortal." Stuart's statement
is consistent with that of Jean Paul Richter, a nineteenth-century
German philosopher: "What a father says to his children is not
heard by the world; but it will be heard by posterity."

In a divorce situation, children often hear different things from
the two parents. To a certain extent, this is probably inevitable. But
on matters that are important, the child should get the same message from each of the parents. This we refer to as consistency in
parent behavior. The reason consistency is so important is that it
makes the child's world more predictable. When things are more
predictable for children, they feel safe, are less anxious, and are less
likely to become angry.

To the child, the adults having authority over him are the main
sources of threat, just as they are the main sources of comfort and
nurturance. If much of the behavior of the adults is consistent and
predictable, the child feels safe. He does not need to spend all of his
energy figuring out what Mom or Dad is going to do next. This frees
the child to concentrate on what other events in his world are predictable. That is, he is free to explore the world and to learn about it.

If children are usually happy, and a joy to be with, their parents have helped to make them that way. If they are usually irritable, fearful, obstinate, or angry, their parents have helped to make them that way. This has not happened knowingly, of course. Parents do, nevertheless, arrange situations in which learnings take place. They do have expectations for children which become self-fulfilling prophecies.

It is mythical to think that somehow children will learn the opposite of what they are taught. Behavior is learned; we do reap what we sow.

Five Ways Emotions Are Used to Achieve Goals

To Get Special Attention

Children (and adults) may use emotions to get special attention. We have all observed situations in which children used emotions to get special attention. Crying is an example of this kind of attention-getting. A child learns from early infancy that someone will meet his every need if he will cry long enough and loudly enough. Most of us, as we grow older, learn to substitute language for crying as the primary means of communicating our wishes. Why do some people, though, continue to use crying and other forms of inappropriate behavior to get attention? The answer is simple: the undesirable behavior continued to work for them. That is, somebody rewarded the child by giving him whatever he demanded, and he continued to use the particular behavior to get what he wanted. It may have seemed easier to the adult to give the child what he wanted than to endure the annoyance of the crying or other attention-getting behavior. Hence, a negative behavior pattern was established.

It is not difficult for most of us to see that this is a logical explanation for a child's developing a number of negative behaviors. We usually think of this kind of behavior in relation to the child as learner. It is just as accurate, however, to think of the child as the teacher and the parent as the learner. Just as surely as the child has learned inappropriate or socially unacceptable ways of behaving, so has the parent learned inappropriate ways of responding to the child. That is, the child has trained the parent to respond in a predictable and (from the child's point of view) rewarding manner. The child gets what he wants, and the adult gets temporary relief from the annoying behavior.

To Control a Situation

Emotions may be used to control a situation or an individual. A temper tantrum is an example of this kind of emotional control. The temper tantrum is usually an emotional show, which means that it requires an audience. Therefore, the most effective procedure for dealing with a temper tantrum is to leave the child alone.

A word of caution for parents: Do not be intimidated by the presence of friends, relatives, or strangers when dealing with a temper tantrum. A "Family Circus" cartoon in the newspaper consisted of two frames. In the first frame the child was attempting to tie his shoe, and the mother said to him, "Crying won't help you get your shoelaces tied." The second frame showed the grandmother in the background as the child walked up to the mother. Tears still falling from his cheeks, and pointing to his shoes, he said: "It did help Mommy! Grandma tied 'em."

Another thing to keep in mind while trying to correct a behavior such as this is that it will always get worse before it gets better. The child will try even harder to employ the technique which has worked so well for him in the past when it appears that it may not now be working. As long as someone gives in, as did the grandmother, the behavior will continue. Patience is the key to success in this situation.

To Retaliate When One Feels Unfairly Treated

A third way in which emotions are used in a negative way is to retaliate for what is thought to be unfair treatment. This is true of adults as well as children—individuals as well as nations. How do you deal with someone who feels that he has been treated unfairly? The question is of particular interest to parents who have more than one child. As any parent knows, an often heard statement in a family is, "It's not fair." The child who is complaining will often be protesting some privilege or perceived advantage another member of the family is receiving.

A parent should not fall into the trap of trying to treat each child just alike. There may be some ways in which all children in a family will be treated alike. There are other ways in which children will not be treated alike, no matter how much they protest. Because of differences in age, maturity, experiences, levels of responsibility, all children will not be treated alike. This fact should be communicated to children with clarity and determination. A child's wishes should be allowed, even when the desired behaviors can't be. The key to this situation is to be a good listener, especially when children are sad, troubled, or bothered. Often listening will mean more to a child than anything else we can do.

For example, when a child brings you a concern over which you have no control (the weather, an activity cancellation, what someone has said) or when you have to confront the child with a limit which has to be set, he is likely to be upset. What he needs more than anything else is for you to accept and understand his feelings at the moment. It is easy for the parent to respond to the child by saying something like, "Do you think I have any control over the weather?" How much more effective it is to say, "I know you are disappointed; you wanted very much to go on the picnic, and it rained." Often nothing more needs to be said. The situation hasn't changed, but the child has had someone acknowledge, understand, and accept his feelings. And when feelings are shared, the load one is carrying may be the same, but it feels lighter.

To Protect One from Functioning

Emotions can be used to protect us from functioning. In extreme cases of severe personality and emotional problems, individuals have lost the use of sight, speech, limbs, and memory and have suffered other physical problems caused from emotional rather than physiological reasons. These severe cases are relatively rare and are not the subject of this discussion.

Our concern here is the much more common occurrences of irrational fears, bizarre behavior, and some physical ailments such as asthma, allergies, vomiting, abdominal pain, and headaches. The reasons for these various problems may be extremely complex. There is no simple explanation. Suggestions will be offered later on how to deal with some of the problems which keep children from functioning normally. It should be noted that any behavior which seems to work for an individual in getting his needs met will continue to be used by him. From the child's point of view he is behaving normally, trying to make sense out of his situation, even though his behavior may be quite socially unacceptable.

To Express Concern or Empathy for Others

We have looked at four ways that emotions are used to achieve goals in a negative way. But emotions are of positive value when they bring to light our concern or empathy for the feelings of others. This increased sensitivity not only improves social relationships, but when we are showing concern for others we feel better about ourselves. Sadly, too many children do not have concern for others modeled for them. Often we allow our fast pace of life to rob us of opportunities to express empathy and concern for others. More than this, such a life-style deprives us of opportunities to translate this concern into deeds of kindness and love. We have to value others enough to make time to empathize with their feelings.

Empathy—like charity, thoughtfulness, kindness, courtesy—must begin at home. We say it must begin in the home because home is where some children are pushed into competition on the basis of personal accomplishments, attractiveness, popularity, school grades, and prominence in organized athletics, almost from infancy.

The point is illustrated beautifully in a poem entitled "In School Days." Whittier pictures a small boy and girl standing in the snow outside a little schoolhouse. The rest of the children were leaving, but these two lingered. The girl had something she wanted to say to the boy. It was simply an apology for spelling a word which caused her to go ahead of him in a spelling bee. Whittier has her say to him:

> "I'm sorry that I spelt the word:
>   I hate to go above you,
> Because,"—the brown eyes lower fell—
>   "Because, you see, I love you!"

A gray-haired man recalls that afternoon and remembers the girl who has now been dead for forty years. Whittier closes the poem with these words:

> He lives to learn, in life's hard school,
>   How few who pass above him
> Lament their triumph and his loss,
>   Like her,—because they love him.

Our experience today is still the same as that of the man in Whittier's poem. Few people have enough empathy to be sad when they succeed and we fail. This is another way of saying that I often do not have sufficient empathy.

Despite the fact that the Education Policies Commission of the National Education Association has identified "Human Relationships" as one of two major goals of education, we still have a long way to go in achieving this. And if we fail in this area, will it really matter that we succeeded in the other? In a 1948 Armistice Day Address, the late General Omar Bradley summarized mankind's condition well when he said, "Ours is a world of nuclear giants and ethical infants. We know more about war than we know about peace, more about killing than we know about living. We have grasped the mystery of the atom and rejected the Sermon on the Mount."

What Does This Mean for Me?

A better understanding of behavior can make the difference between being a happy, successful parent and a frustrated, defeated parent. Or a happy, successful teacher and a frustrated teacher. Or a joyous church leader and a befuddled one. If you don't like yourself the way you are, you can change. It is never too late to begin again. Every day one should take a long, careful look at oneself and try to change those things that need changing and strengthen those qualities that should remain. If there are behaviors in the child which you would like to change, it is more economical in time, energy, and resources to look first at your own behavior and see if these are things which first could be changed in yourself.

Many minor day-to-day problems can be prevented if the household is thoughtfully organized, if responsibilities are shared, and if lines of communication are kept open between parent and child.

A significant reward for a parent's efforts is to see cooperative and responsive children develop into caring adults. Perhaps becoming an understanding, honest, encouraging parent is like seeking truth and beauty—a goal worth pursuing even if one's chances of achieving it are slim.

Newspaper and magazine articles—even events in your own school system—have probably made you aware that discipline is a major problem for teachers in the nation's schools. Many of us who are parents can identify with this concern of teachers, for we are also faced with discipline to some extent almost daily. If you are a divorced parent, then you know the extent to which this is true in your own experience.

One reason misbehavior is such a common occurrence among children is that this is a sure way to get parents, teachers, and others to notice them. Misbehavior is the price we pay for failing to give children the recognition they deserve for the positive things they do. It is almost an axiom that "A misbehaving child is a discouraged child." It is the goal of this chapter, then, to offer help in

5.
Managing
Children's
Behavior

What Is Discipline?

Everyone who talks about discipline doesn't necessarily understand the meaning of it. The word *discipline* comes from the same Latin word which means *pupil*. So, the basic idea involved in discipline is learning. A disciplined person is one who learns—from himself and from others. We would like to make the distinction between discipline and punishment. When the word *discipline* is mentioned, the first thing that many of us think about is punishment. We shall discuss punishment later, but our focus now is on the truer meaning of the word: a learner, learning.

Learning is a mixture of joy and sadness. That is, each of us learns from pleasant experiences as well as from unpleasant experiences. Adults should not try to make everything pleasant for children. Not many people (none that we know) have discovered an exciting, joyous way to teach the multiplication tables, for example. The point being made is that teaching and learning take place all of the time, not just when we feel good about something.

Increasingly, all of us as parents hope we can provide our children with opportunities for joyful and exciting learning. We know full well, however, that some of a person's most significant learnings are associated with pain, struggle, and adversity. In fact, this discovery is in itself a significant learning for children. Discipline can be thought of as the learnings which tend to be related to these difficult experiences.

Discipline addresses itself to the most crucial challenge of being a parent—teaching children increasingly to take responsibility for their own lives. As we help our children embrace self-discipline, we are helping them acquire one of the most significant learnings in life. Albert Einstein put it another way: "Education is that which remains, even if one has forgotten everything he learned in school."

Self-discipline is the ability to hear commands that are unpleasant, to see tasks that need to be done, to smell the aroma of toil, to taste the bitterness of persistence, to feel the agony of effort, and to carry through with actions undertaken. Discipline is doing what needs to be done, when it needs to be done, whether you feel like doing it or not.

Three Essentials for Success

Assuming physical needs are met, every person needs three things in order to be healthy and successful in life. First, he needs a value identity (I am important—to myself and others). Every person needs someone to believe in him—someone to believe that he can become more than he now is.

Secondly, each person should have a reliable source of love. The human infant and child is the most dependent of all infants and young among the animal species and requires the most continuing adult, authoritative love in order to survive. This love is communicated through time spent with the child, through physical contact (more than just hugging and kissing), and through the words that we say.

And words are more than sounds and symbols. They are sounds and symbols, to be sure, but they are much more. The words we speak and the words we hear help to shape our lives. Emperor Frederick, who ruled the Holy Roman Empire in the twelfth century, conducted a crude experiment. For some reason he wanted to know what man's original language was. Would it be more natural for an untutored child to speak Hebrew, Greek, or Latin? He reasoned that if he could isolate infants from birth from any human voices, they would eventually speak in the tongue most natural to man. He arranged for a group of infants to be reared by wet nurses, who were instructed to maintain silence in the presence of the infants. The women did as they were told, in spite of their natural inclination to speak to the infants. The infants never heard a word. Within several months they were all dead.[1]

Our personality is being formed and deformed by the words that we hear; we are continually being shaped by what others communicate to us. Jesus was aware of this when he interpreted the Commandment "Thou shalt not kill" (Matt. 5:21) to cover words spoken in anger. Many of us know that a verbal blow can be as damaging to the personality as a physical blow is damaging to the body.

A person who knows that God loves him and that others love him can overcome almost any obstacle that life offers.

Third, in order to be healthy and successful one needs to have a sense of meaning and purpose for his life. A proverb which captures this truth, says, "No wind blows well for the ship without a port." While we cannot set goals for our children or anyone else, we can be available to offer guidance and encouragement as our children discover their talents and seek to develop them to their maximum potential. Every child needs to feel that he is loved not because of what he can do, how intelligent he is, how handsome or beautiful he or she is, how well he may perform in some area that we value, but that he is loved unconditionally. The child needs to know that he is loved without strings attached, simply because of the unique and special person that he or she is. When a child discovers that he is the object of deep interest and pride, and that this is not related to his performance in any way, he begins to feel that he is a person of some worth and that life does have meaning for him.

What Every Child Needs Most

You may wonder what this topic has to do with behavior. It has everything to do with behavior. When these basic personality needs are not met, children respond in some predictable, and usually socially unacceptable, ways. It is our belief that this feeling of self-worth, self-esteem, or whatever we may choose to call this attitude of mind, is what every child needs most. Self-esteem is not the opposite of being humble; it is how a person feels about himself. If a person has low self-esteem, he is going to have problems and is going to cause problems for other people. For the remainder of this chapter we shall focus on some of the most common reactions of children and what we can do to help them, when self-esteem is lacking.

Please remember two things. First, these reactions are characteristic of all children, not just children of divorce. Second, our focus is only on some of the most common ways that children act when they do not feel good about themselves. We are not saying that the lack of self-esteem is the sole cause of all discipline problems. Obviously, there are other reasons for such problems, some of which may be medically treated. However, the overwhelming majority of behavior problems relate primarily to self-esteem, or how a child views himself, his worth, his abilities, his uniqueness.

We are all happy and sad at different times in our lives. Happiness and sadness are as much a part of life as night and day. We want to be happy; we want to feel good about ourselves. The truth is, though, there are times when we are sad and when we think too little of ourselves. The actions which characterize children with low self-esteem become a concern only when they are repeated continually and over a long period of time (several weeks or more).

To the casual observer, it might seem that we have placed a great deal of emphasis upon self-esteem. But consider one example of many studies in this area. Philip Shaver and Carin Rubenstein analyzed several thousand responses to surveys conducted in several cities in the United States. They found that people whose parents were divorced are lonelier as adults than people from intact families. Reporting on their findings, Rubenstein said: "We found that children of divorce had lower self-esteem than those whose parents had remained together. The younger the person was when the parents divorced, the lower the person's self-esteem and the more lonely he was as an adult."[2]

Common Characteristics of Children with Low Self-Esteem

Timidity

The timid child may be fearful and shy. Timidity is normal, to some extent, in the preschool child. We should take timidity seriously if it continues beyond grade school (the sixth or seventh grade). The caution for parents is not to thrust a child into social situations until he is ready for them. If a child relates well to other members of the family, he can be counted on, in his own good time, to be ready for parties, summer camp, and other activities with children his own age. Most of us are so anxious for our children to do well that we are tempted to insist that the clay of our child's personality conform to our own vision of what he or she *ought* to be. Because of our emotional involvement, we can easily convince ourselves that we possess the gift of seeing what promise a child has, that we possess a secret blueprint for his or her growth. When we are able to separate our wishes from the realities of what is best for the child, we then see life itself. We share in the unfolding of a life outside our own. We love, rather than use, the person who is the object of our affection.

A shy, timid child often does not come to the attention of parents and teachers simply because he "has no problem." In reality, this child may be experiencing more difficulty than one who is constantly causing trouble. If this withdrawal persists over a long period of time, help from a pastor or someone else outside the family may be indicated.

Bullying

When a child's primary way of relating to those around him is through bullying and bragging, he is telling us that he does not feel good about himself. He needs to convince himself and others that he is more than he appears to be. This child usually wants attention. Some have called bullying "puffer-fish behavior." The small puffer fish has the ability to blow himself up to twice his normal size, or more.

A father, describing his child's behavior, said, "I hate a bully, and every time my child acts this way I punish him, but this doesn't seem to help." The father in this case was a busy insurance executive who had little time to spend with his family. As desperate as it may seem, puffer-fish behavior was the way the boy had learned that he could definitely get his father's attention.

We have all seen children deliberately do things for which they knew they would be punished. Why will children continue to do such things, even in the face of severe punishment? The answer is simply this: Any kind of attention, though it be negative, is better than no attention. The challenge for parents is to help the child find constructive ways of gaining attention. When he does something which is praiseworthy, let him know it immediately. We are all prone to point out a child's negative traits and then neglect to compliment him for his positive behaviors.

The Two Faces of Anger

The angry child will usually react in one of two ways. He will attack (objects, animals, or people) in a direct, physical way; or he will use a more subtle, passive way of showing anger and displeasure. Again, we are not talking about the occasional periods of anger which are normal for everyone. Rather, we are speaking of anger which persists over a period of time and is a constant way of life.

One explanation for this behavior is that the child is modeling the actions of those closest to him, usually the parents. He is doing as they do, not as they say. As parents, we tend to dislike in our children those things which are problems for us. If we are honest with ourselves, we can often discover some of our major problem areas by observing the behaviors of our children which upset us most. If anger is a problem for us, for example, then this is a behavior of our child which we will likely dislike most. So, in a sense, if there are behaviors in our children which we would like to change, we should first look at ourselves and see if these are behaviors of our own which we could better try to change.

Why is it that the behaviors of our children which are most upsetting to us are also the things which are the biggest problems to us? One explanation is that, in many ways, our children are extensions of our own personalities. And when we see in our children negative traits and characteristics most like us, we panic. Our immediate reaction is that we will not tolerate this in the child, and he or she must change. The irony is that in our effort to help the child, we model for him the very behavior we wish to eliminate. We do not help a child deal with anger by becoming angry ourselves. We do not teach a child honesty by being dishonest. We do not teach a child politeness in a rude manner. We do not teach a child patience by being impatient with him. On and on the list goes.

In addition to modeling the behavior of parents, another explanation for a child's negative actions is that he is trying to feel more adequate by making someone else feel less adequate. When a child really begins to feel better about himself, he will have less need to be angry and unhappy.

It is not unusual to see children react by showing the other face of anger: being passive. Sometimes these children are referred to as "passive-aggressive." This term simply means that a child's primary way of showing his anger is not in an open, boisterous manner. These children often appear to be free of all feelings of anger because they are not showing anger in the way that most of us expect to see it. It is not unusual to see middle-class and upper middle-class children react in this way. For example, we have observed children who would choose to fail in school despite a good background and a high intelligence. Oh, they did not consciously choose this outcome in the sense of sitting down and saying, "As a way of getting back at my parents, I am going to fail in school." But the results were just the same—that is what they chose to do. A father or mother may not have time for his or her child, but a way that the child can command attention is to fail in some area the parent values highly—like school. This is an attention-getting type of failure which is often associated with children of higher socioeconomic backgrounds. It is not uncommon for these children to have many of the material things which money can buy, and yet be deprived— deprived of the personal interest and time of their parents.

If a child is normal or above normal in intelligence, and yet failing, his failure may be caused for other reasons. We shall discuss some of these later.

Unsure About Decisions

Children who are lacking in self-confidence will find decision-making difficult. One way to build a child's self-confidence is to provide him with appropriate opportunities for making choices. This can begin early in the child's life by providing him with two choices at a time, either of which will be acceptable to us. There is no question about who is in control, but when the child chooses, he grows more than when we decide for him. If many opportunities have not been provided for children to make choices when they are young, we can't expect them to deal successfully with choices when they are older.

Another factor contributing to a child's inability to make decisions is the poor model of the parents. If parents find it difficult to make decisions, this certainly will be caught by the children. If a child makes a wrong decision and is repeatedly rebuked by his parents, he may conclude that the safest and easiest way to please his parents is to make no decisions at all.

A child should be helped to see that wrong decisions are not necessarily failures, but simply mistakes from which one can learn. Children should be brought in on family discussions about problems which affect all of the family. When parents occasionally make a wrong decision, this matter should be discussed also. A child should see that no one is expected to be perfect. He can learn from his own mistakes as well as our mistakes as parents.

Attitude of Failure

Some children are able to make decisions well enough, but they make unrealistic ones. With the aid and assistance of parents who are trying to have the child meet the parents' needs, they often set goals which are beyond their capacities to achieve. It is devastating for a child not to have someone to believe in him, but it is also frustrating for the child to have somebody push him to succeed in an area beyond his aspirations and abilities. The child should not feel that he is being manipulated by the parents to achieve *their* goals, but is being encouraged to accomplish *his* goals. The vision of one man does not lend itself to another. Each person has to have his own dream, live his own life, see his own vision.

It is easy for us to expect more than we should of our children, or to impose our goals on them. Also, it is extremely easy to develop a pattern of responding to children in a negative way. We do it all of the time because our society has a bent toward being negative. Proof of this is that children learn to say no before they learn to say yes. So, you see, we need to be careful about the use of the general words, *always, never, certain*, and similar words, when used in association with negative comments about children. "Do you always have to drop things?" "Can you never do anything right?" "You are certain to make a mess of things when you do them yourself," and similar comments help to develop an expectation of failure in a child.

Children who have a negative picture of themselves, and who have an expectation of failure, tend to regard a single failure as characteristic of the kind of person they are. Children with a positive self-concept tend to view a single failure as an isolated incident. On the positive side of this issue is the fact that self-concept, like any other learned behavior, can be changed or be unlearned. It is not an easy task, and the changing of self-concept must begin with the significant others. If a child is convinced that he is no good, can't do school work, is not loved, can't make friends, or whatever—this negative self-concept can be changed. Be prepared, though, for such a change to take time and patient understanding.

No Joy for Tomorrow

If a person is to have an adequate view of himself, he must view himself as a child of God. Once a person becomes convinced that he is loved by God and by others who are important to him, he is well on his way to becoming the kind of person who interacts with others in a healthy and productive manner. He will know who he is, where he is going, and why he is here. He will then be able to make sense out of life instead of viewing the future with alarm and doubt. The child who finds order, security, and love within the home will see that he counts for something outside the home as well. He will experience joy today and will know there will always be some left for tomorrow. Children who become independent and successful usually come from homes which demand strict accountability and responsibility. Children want limits and structure. When we deprive them of this, we give them the message that they are not valued.

Five Parent Behaviors for Improving Self-Concept

Praise Appropriately

One of the ways to help a child improve his self-concept, or to feel better about himself, is to praise him appropriately. Maybe one of the best ways to ensure that we will praise a child appropriately is to understand what is meant by inappropriate praise. First of all, praise that evaluates a child's personality tends to be destructive. To tell a child how good he is or how bad he is is to praise judgmentally or with evaluation. Why is it undesirable to praise judgmentally? The best reason is that it is not helpful. Judgmental praise may cause the child to become anxious, be dependent, and even result in his becoming defensive. We want children to acquire the opposite characteristics: to be self-reliant, self-directed, and self-controlled. These qualities develop as a result of reliance on inner motivation and evaluation, not from outside judgment. If a child is to be himself, he must be free from praise which evaluates his character traits. One reason evaluative praise of conduct is so undesirable is that it conveys the idea that we are surprised at "good" behavior because we expected "bad" behavior. Children often live up to our expectations, whether those expectations are stated or implied.

On the other hand, praise that is appropriate appreciates, describes children's efforts and accomplishments, and expresses our feelings about them. Praise should be sincere. To praise a child falsely is worse than not praising a child at all. Allow your child to overhear you tell someone else how good he or she is. When we compliment a child in this way, we bolster his belief in himself.

For example, one of the problems many parents have with teenagers is getting them to honor the time that they agree to return home in the evening. If a child has never had to be responsible in this way before, then he will not act as responsibly as a child who has learned to respect time from childhood, in a hundred different ways. The child who has learned this lesson from childhood may have been given time limits for brushing his teeth, cleaning his room, going out to play, visiting a neighbor, or so forth. Over time, privileges would have been given or denied based upon the child's conforming to the limits.

Too, we need to keep in mind that praise is not simply what we say to the child. It is that, but in addition it is what he says to himself. When our words state what we like and appreciate about the child's efforts, his help, his work, his accomplishments—then the child draws his own conclusions about himself.

We have already discussed in chapter 2 the importance of the developmental stage of ages three through six. This stage is also important in relation to self-esteem. Unless a child already has considerable confidence in his abilities, he needs praise at this stage just to help him build up his self-esteem. If we forget everything else about praise, we should remember this: Praise should describe without evaluating personality and report without judging character.

Praise Yourself

It may seem a little strange that we should advise parents to praise themselves. Actually, it is most desirable when one realizes the value of this simple behavior. By allowing your child to hear you praise yourself, you provide a good model of self-concept. It is much more likely that a child will feel good about himself and his accomplishments if his parent feels good about himself and his accomplishments.

Self-praise, on the part of the parent or the child, is simply being realistic and honest about yourself. As we share our strengths and good points, we need to communicate the feeling that we are happy being who we are.

We bolster a person's self-esteem when we help him realize that he is made in God's image. A child will reflect the behavior we mirror back to him.

Teach Children to Praise Themselves

As a child moves into adolescence, he has to use a self-praise system if he is to be successful. As a child becomes more and more independent of his parents, increasingly he has to rely on his own resources. In the process of learning how to praise himself, a child also learns how to respect his opinion of himself and does not need the affirming approval of the crowd like a person who is less sure of his own strengths and abilities. The transition from childhood to adolescence is made easier when children are given appropriate responsibilities during their younger years. One cannot wait for a child to enter his youth before giving him appropriate responsibilities. Many parents do not give their children responsibility until they enter their youth only to discover, sure enough, that their children cannot act responsibly. On the other hand, if responsibility has been given to a child all along, he will have learned how to praise himself and be praised in a responsible way.

Teach Children to Praise Others

As a child learns how to praise himself, he is also going to learn how to praise others. These keys to helping a child develop a better self-concept are all related. Each builds upon the other and strengthens the other. Like most behaviors, a parent's modeling of this behavior is one of the most effective methods of teaching. The child who often hears his parents praise others is much more likely to praise others himself. This kind of praise should also be nonevaluative.

Self-concept is learned, and it is changing continually. By teaching a child to praise others we will be helping him to improve his self-concept. We cannot look for and admire qualities in others without wanting some of those same qualities for ourselves.

Help Children Evaluate Themselves Realistically

Children usually evaluate themselves unrealistically. In a sense, children are always incompetent. That is, their rate of learning is high, but they have not had the time or experience to acquire many of the skills that are desirable for successful living. Often, instead of a child's getting praised for what he does well or for his sincere effort, he gets criticized for not being perfect. A parent's standard for his child may be so high that it is impossible for the child to achieve it.

Realistic evaluation and goal setting are opposite sides of the same coin. Children are able to participate in goal setting and should be given this opportunity from time to time. A parent must realize that he cannot demand perfection at first. Growth and maturity are slow and continuous processes, whether we are talking about an oak tree or a child.

Five Techniques for Managing Behavior

When child behavior is being discussed, people who are interested in children will listen politely. After everything has been said, some brave person will usually comment: "That sounds good. But what are some specific things that I can do to better manage my child's behavior?" We give the answer in the form of an acrostic: CHARM them.

Consistency
Hierarchy of responses
Always make enforceable limits
Respect the dignity of the individual child
Maximize opportunities for children to make choices

Consistency

Children are skilled in manipulating situations in their own behalf. Our behavioral messages should be the same as our verbal messages. In other words, as adults related to children each of us should do what he says he will do. We call this intrapersonal consistency. Too, there should be interpersonal consistency. That is, the child should get the same message from each authority with whom he interacts. Holding behavioral expectations consistent makes life more enjoyable for us and the child.

Too, there should be consistency in the way we communicate behavioral expectations. If a child is doing something which annoys a parent, the child should not have to be told five or six times to stop the behavior. Often, however, particularly if a parent is busy, he or she may tell the child five or six times to do something or stop doing something while the parent continues with his own activity. Over a period of time it is likely that the child in such a situation will learn that the parent does not mean business the first or second time.

To help a child prepare for a task that may be unpleasant, give the child some lead time. Tell him, for example, that in five minutes it will be time to prepare for bed. One minute before time you may want to say that he has only one more minute. The command "Prepare for bed" should be given only once.

Hierarchy of Responses

We need to have a hierarchy of responses in managing the behavior of children. That is, more severe techniques are always preceded by less severe techniques. Just as you do not use a cannon to kill a mouse, neither do you use any form of discipline which is more severe than necessary to get the job done. If a disapproving look can give the child a message that his behavior is unacceptable, then you do not need to speak to him. If speaking to a child in the normal tone of voice will communicate your message, then you do not need to raise your voice.

Knowing and practicing a variety of responses to children can make life more enjoyable for parent and child. More severe techniques are reserved for more severe situations.

A couple of techniques you may wish to try in responding to children:

Lower your voice as a child becomes louder. (You do not teach children control by being out of control yourself.)

Do not try to reason with a child when he is out of control. Simply say to the child that you will discuss the matter when he is in control.

Always Make Enforceable Limits

No matter how much children protest to the contrary, they want and need the security of consistent limits. Having reasonable limits for children is one way that we communicate our love for them. We have observed some adoptive parents who were reluctant to impose limits on their children for fear that the adoptive children would interpret such limits as their not loving them. The sad truth is, the children draw just the opposite conclusion. They feel that if the parents really loved them they would impose definite limits on their behavior.

As necessary as limits and rules are, their number should be as few as possible. Too many "don'ts" give some children ideas. For example, a child may never think of sticking beans up his nose if no one makes a rule about it. Too, children are more inclined to obey the rules that they have had a part in making, just as an adult is more apt to wake up by an alarm that he has set rather than by one someone else has set.

Finally, if a rule cannot be enforced, it is better not to have the rule. For if a child can violate one rule, we are extending an invitation for him to violate other rules.

Respect the Dignity of the Individual Child

Whatever technique you use in controlling children, a cardinal rule to remember is this: Always respect the dignity of the individual child. A technique may seem to work, but it is not a good one if it violates this principle. Human dignity must be guarded; good taste is extremely important. The integrity of the individual is always maintained. Generally speaking, you praise in public and censure in private.

One way that you show respect for the dignity of children is to let them know that you value them. You let children know that you value them by spending time with them. Sadly, we acknowledge that many parents are not friends with their children. Over the years they have formed the habit of ignoring a child when the child is upset and punishing him/her when the parents are upset. Incidentally, children know that punishment is rarely administered for their benefit; rather, it serves the needs of the punishing adult.

The parent whose sole way of controlling children is through punishment is perpetuating a cycle of aggression which is passed from one generation to the next. The extreme illustration of this is child abuse. Increasingly, child abuse cases are being brought to light and are having to be dealt with by society.

In desperation many parents will often resort to blame, shame, reproach, rebuke, threat, and punishment. Not only do these methods not guard the dignity of the child, they fail to correct.

Maximize Opportunities for Children to Make Choices

Providing a child with alternatives or choices is better than arbitrarily deciding for him. When you give a child an opportunity to choose, you help his self-concept to grow just a little. A parent can give a child choices without abdicating his or her responsibilities as parent. After all, deciding who decides is more important than who decides.

Independence must be encouraged if you want to develop responsibility. However, when limits are broken you take away some of the opportunity for independent action. You then return to the child the appropriate responsibility as he is able to handle it.

When you give children choices, you invite cooperation. The reason for this is that you are making them less dependent, and dependency tends to breed resentment and anger. In a hundred small ways from day to day, you can give a child the opportunity to make choices.

What Does This Mean for Me?

In a real sense, we cannot manage or control someone else's behavior. As has already been stated, the only authority we have over the behavior of another is the control we have over our own behavior. The techniques you have considered in this chapter, coupled with a better understanding of your own behavior, can certainly help you relate to others—particularly your children—in a more positive and growth-producing way.

These techniques, when applied, can change your life. Someone has said that Christianity has not been tried and found wanting; it has been found difficult and not tried. One of the lyrics in *The Sound of Music* says that "Nothing comes from nothing—nothing never could." Life's greatest rewards are reserved for life's greatest challenges. Surely being a good parent is one of these.

"Seems like I spend all my time counseling people who are either divorced or about to divorce." The pastor slumped into a chair, hand over his eyes.

"I know what you mean," his friend responded. *"It seems like all of our friends are falling apart."*

The pastor sat in thought a moment. Hands clasped between his knees, he continued, *"The truth is our church needs to find more ways to help families in this situation. I try, but there has to be some other way."*

Other ways to help are the primary subject of this chapter. It is designed for any person who has responsibility as a church staff member; but most of all it is for

6.
Professional Children's Workers in Church Settings

When we talk about professional children's workers, we have in mind a special group. We include men and women who are following God's call to make ministry to children from birth through elementary school their life's work. Some of these people made this commitment early in youth or in young adult years. Others made the commitment much later. While many responded to a Damascus Road sort of call, others moved into their present positions a step at a time, not knowing just where the road would lead.

We salute them all. And we do so because we have seen the quality of their dedication to Christ, his church, and to children. We do so because we have felt their love and concern. We do so because they are willing to pay the price to provide the help children and parents need. So this chapter is dedicated with loving appreciation to every church staff member who seeks to help children and their families.

This chapter suggests guidelines for planning and conducting training opportunities designed to help both parents and children who are affected by divorce. It also contains guidelines for planning and conducting training opportunities for church workers involved with divorced persons and their children. In addition, the chapter calls attention to some community resources which can be helpful to the church staff member as he plans such activities and as he helps families on an individual basis.

We have divided the chapter according to the groups of persons for whom training opportunities can be provided. We will begin with church workers, move to parents, and then to children. This order is not intended to suggest a sequence of events to be followed in a particular congregation. The group with which a professional worker should begin depends upon the needs in his or her situation.

Helping Church Workers

We referred elsewhere to teachers and leaders in church organization as "first line." These men and women are, as a rule, closer to boys and girls than any other persons in the church. Their support to a child in any emotional crisis is, to the child, the expression of the church family's love for him. This expression of love may be improved if a worker has a good understanding of divorce and its effect upon a child.

Chapter 3 examines some of the attitudes likely held by persons who work with children in church settings. Please take a minute to review that portion of chapter 3 before you continue reading this chapter. With those needs in mind, let's take a look at some

Needs of Church Workers

Identification of their feelings toward divorce, toward divorced or divorcing parents, and toward children of divorce.—There is no one "right" attitude toward divorce, not in a moral sense. So workers do not need to be brainwashed into accepting a certain attitude toward divorce. They do need to examine their attitudes in order to better understand how these attitudes affect their work with the children in their organizations.

Understanding of basic Bible teachings about the family.—Much space in the Bible is devoted to families and events in their lives. Additional space is devoted to teachings about the family, both in the Old and New Testaments. And many of these events and teachings are incorporated in most church curriculums used with preschoolers and children of elementary-school age. Workers, however, need to take an adult-level look at these teachings, rather than merely to approach them with the idea of transmitting them to children at their level.

Understanding of their church's stance on divorce.—All Christian communities endorse the concept of lifelong commitment to one person as the framework for homemaking and child rearing. Within that framework, official church positions vary. In fact, in denominations which emphasize the autonomy of local congregations, the stance of one congregation within that denomination may vary significantly from the stance of another congregation. In some denominations, no official stance exists beyond "We hold what the Bible teaches."

Individuals in a congregation may be ignorant of what their church holds—even if an official position does exist. In a loosely-knit denomination, individual church members may be unaware of resolutions adopted by their national agencies and commissions. Such a person can easily be caught short when someone with more information challenges him.

None of this discussion is meant to overrule the right of a person to interpret the Bible for himself. We do wish to underscore the importance of a person's knowing what is going on in relation to divorce.

Understanding of the divorce picture within the church family and the community.—It is easy to ignore what we do not wish to see. We can be impressed with the large number of singles-again we see through their classroom door at church. At the same time, we can be oblivious to the problems they represent. An individual teacher may be acutely conscious of the divorce of the parents of one child in his small group of six or seven and never dream how many other children in his church also come from broken homes.

Insights into the problems of parents and children of divorce.—Knowing that a child comes from a single-parent family is one thing. Appreciation for the feelings he is likely to be experiencing is another. Yet a lack of such appreciation and understanding hampers even the most loving and willing of workers.

Definition of his own role in relation to the family and the child.—The people who work with children in a church often lack a clear-cut definition of their work. They know they are to "teach the lesson," "try to get everyone to come every Sunday," and "try to reach the boys and girls who don't go to Sunday School anywhere." They may not have given much thought to their role as supporters of the family in crisis.

This aspect of their work involves two primary relationships. The first is their relationship to the child they teach. He or she comes first. While the teacher or leader must never let himself become an ally of the child against the parent, his first concern ought to be the child.

The second relationship is closely bound to the first. It is the teacher's relationship to the parent. Although this parent may be ministered to by adult teachers, he may not be a part of any class or department nor be a member of the church. In this case, the child's worker provides the parent's only church tie. What the teacher of the child says and does becomes the witness of the church and her Lord to that parent. Just how this relationship develops depends upon many personal factors—both those of the teacher and the parent.

Possible Types of Training

In this section of the chapter the main emphasis will be upon the content for training sessions. Almost any body of content can be used in a variety of settings. A one-hour seminar can take place at the end of a social hour. It can also be incorporated into an evening which provides several electives. The same content can be part of a Sunday afternoon or evening session, or it can be scheduled for a weeknight or a morning.

Several bodies of content can be incorporated into one course. The course can be offered on four or five consecutive evenings. It can be offered one session per week for four or five weeks. All of such a course or major segments of it might form a retreat program for one day or an evening and morning.

Preliminary to all of these training sessions ought to be the offering of one or more courses dealing with basics in understanding children. Such an offering is essential because one does not develop an understanding of the child of divorce in a vacuum. A child is first of all a child, and secondarily a child in certain conditions or with certain limitations. Many denominational presses offer such books in connection with their curriculum offerings.

Identification of feelings.—This subject is probably one of the two most difficult areas of need listed earlier. Unless a proper climate exists, people in our society generally find talking about inner feelings rather difficult. This tendency becomes more pronounced as one begins to deal with feelings the subjects find hard to define or which they think may be judged unsuitable by the group. The purpose of a session(s) dealing with this area must be only to explore persons' feelings, not to induce "right" feelings or to get the persons involved to concede that they ought to feel a certain way.

Obviously, a session of this type requires consummate skill on the part of the leader. For one thing, he or she will deal with some workers who are themselves divorced. He will most surely be dealing with some workers who are defensive about divorce within their families or among their close friends.

Content for such a session can be built off of the case studies included in the appendix to this book. After a consideration of the feelings of children who are reacting to divorce, the group might be

open to sharing personal feelings about divorce. This sharing can be
followed by discussing how these feelings affect one's relationship
with children and parents. A sensitive leader will know when continuing the discussion might do more damage than good.

Understanding basic Bible teachings.—Content for this area is probably available from the publisher of material used by your church
organizations. Another source of material is units used in your Sunday School. From time to time adult study units focus on basic Bible
teachings about the family. Since those who work with children seldom get exposure to these units, one of them previously studied or
currently in use by adult Sunday School classes can be effective content.

Who should teach such a course? Other things being equal, the
better the teacher's Bible scholarship the better the study. For this
reason, the pastor or some other seminary-trained person should
teach the class. Another psychological advantage is gained if the
teacher is also recognized as someone who has a happy family life.
Example goes a long way.

Understanding the church's stance on divorce.—This is the other highly
sensitive topic from our list of needs. The tone of such sessions in
most congregations probably needs to be more informative than
authoritative. That is, the teacher should introduce class members
to the major documents which contain the statements to which they
need exposure without demanding that they give their personal endorsement to the statements. Some persons may disagree with the
statements initially and may need to verbalize that resistance even
though they later embrace the view expressed in the documents. To
demand "obedience" to these statements can be a major tactical
error.

In many situations the pastor will be the best person to handle
this content. His position within the church family lends credibility
to what needs to be said. However, he must not feel threatened if
people are vocal about their mistrust of statements made by denominational bodies—or even those made by local church fathers!

Consider this sequencing of content areas: first, the Bible teachings regarding the family and then the church's stance on divorce.
Assuming that the church's statements are rooted in the Bible, this
sequence will help workers better understand the statements.

The divorce picture in the church and community.—Obviously the content for this session(s) must be tailored for a particular congregation. This fact indicates the wisdom of the church staff's gathering the data. Church records will reveal data about church families. Community agencies or state agencies can supply statistical data applicable to a community in general. Secular magazines and family magazines published by denominations can supply some information. And, of course, the first chapter of this book contains useful material.

In presenting the material dealing with the congregation, tact is the first rule. Nothing is gained by dropping the bombshell that everybody's ideal couple has just become a statistic.

The picture of divorce for this session can be presented by a church staff member. The children's worker may prefer to serve as host or hostess and invite another church staff member to be the presenter. We do not say "speaker" since no one wants to sit still for an hour of statistics. A well-trained church staff member should remember to use good group-learning techniques, including discussion and visuals.

Problems of parents and children.—The appendix to this book is a good resource. Some portions of it may be used with only slight adjustment to fit the group. The case studies, for instance, can be invaluable.

An additional approach is a symposium of divorced persons. They must be persons who can deal fairly objectively with their experience. No still bitter person should be given a platform for getting even with an ex-mate, the church, or society in general. The session can include a question-and-answer time if this arrangement is not too threatening to the participants. The session need not be rehearsed as if it were a play, but the participants and the moderator (probably the children's worker on the staff) should share what they intend to do.

It is possible that some older youths who weathered the divorce experience as younger children could participate. Including children in the panel is probably too risky for the children. A series of role plays (under solid guidance) is another workable alternative. Avoid using a role play which is so specific that the group will think you are dealing with a certain couple or family. Also be wary of thinly disguised cases.

Definition of role.—Content for this session can be based on organizational guidelines followed in conducting children's work in your church. The group can consider their job descriptions. In the course of exploring these descriptions, focus attention upon those statements which refer specifically to or imply responsibility for the emotional needs of children and their parents. Move from this focus to discussion of the implications which group members see for their work with children of divorce and their parents.

Such a session is best led by the professional staff member. It might be led by a department director with status among his peers, or a "neutral" from another congregation might be brought in. Of course, this person must have good training and sound experience in children's work in church settings.

Another possibility is to integrate this session into a total training program. Resource material for this program can be the organizational manual your denomination publishes as a guide for church work with children.

Helping Divorced Parents

In a sense, the children's worker on a church staff is not responsible for parents, though in some congregations such a dual responsibility may be assigned to one person. Nevertheless, a conscientious children's worker accepts the challenge of helping parents if he or she wishes to help children. This responsibility can often be discharged best through cooperative work with church staff members who work with adults. For this reason, most of the suggestions in this section of the chapter need to be implemented in cooperation with the staff person responsible for adults.

Needs of Divorced Parents

Acceptance by others.—In spite of the reduction of stigma attached to divorce, many divorced persons feel acutely that their larger families, their children, and their friends disapprove of them. The objective fact may be that family, children, and friends do react negatively to what the divorced person has done. The divorced person is likely to view this disapproval as rejection of him as a person, though in fact, others may still hold him in high regard.

Some divorced persons seem to feel this sense of rejection most strongly in relation to the church. "You just don't fit in anywhere anymore," one middle-aged divorcee said with resignation. Yet she was active in the singles-again group in her church, one of the largest and most active singles-again groups in her state.

For this reason, it is important that divorced parents feel accepted as worthy persons by church staff members. Obviously, there is a limit to which a church staff member can go in "proving" to an insecure person that he or she is accepted. In extreme cases, such persons are unable to receive acceptance no matter how it is expressed.

Those who teach children in church organizations should also assume some responsibility for helping divorced parents feel accepted. In the earlier part of this chapter, we have explored some factors which affect workers and their ability to accept parents who are divorced.

Self-understanding.—This need goes beyond an understanding of the person's immediate situation. And it is a need which is shared by all person—single-again or never married.

Clarification of their personal situation.—Just because a person is divorced is no assurance that he has a clear concept of his situation. From a practical viewpoint, he or she may not, for instance, understand even his or her legal rights. The fault is not necessarily some lawyer's. In a time of trauma many persons simply do not think clearly. Some persons are so determined to cut the marriage ties, believing that doing so is the only route to peace, that they pay scant attention to legal details.

Even among those who do understand the legal aspects of divorce, some have not carefully appraised their current situations. Such may be the case with either the parent who keeps the children and remains in the home or with the parent who leaves the family. For example, one or both of the parties may still be trying to maintain their former standard of living although expenses have risen sharply because two households, not one, must be maintained. Even the cost of the divorce itself may have cut sharply into family resources.

A divorced parent may still cherish the illusion that somehow the whole world can yet be set back where it was in the time of his or her greatest happiness. He (or she) may not consciously believe that the departed mate will return, but he is not yet ready to pick up the pieces of life and to go forward. Such a person tends to look backward rather than forward.

Understanding of the child of divorce.—One divorced mother remarked to a counselor: "I don't think that the divorce has affected Teddy. Not at all. We have kept the same routines as before. And besides he never mentions his father." An unaffected four-year-old who never mentions the father he had adored a year before!

Many divorced parents have little or no idea of the common feelings of children of divorce, those feelings detailed in chapter 2. When they spend a little time thinking about the child's feelings which can be expected to flow normally from divorce, they are amazed. And, as a rule they are also relieved.

Even deeper than the problem of not understanding the effects of divorce on a child, many divorced parents—and others, too—have little understanding of children in general. Becoming a parent does not automatically qualify one for parenting over the long haul. Like all parents, the divorced parent needs basic understanding of the stages and phases of childhood.

Goals for the future.—Even those divorced parents who have determined to put aside the burden of the past and to move resolutely into the future may need help in developing realistic goals. Long-range consideration of such matters as the education of the children require attention and planning. The divorced parent may need to consider furthering or redirecting his own education or training in order to qualify for a better-paying position.

Understanding of what the Bible teaches about divorce and of their church's or denomination's stance on divorce.—This need is virtually the same as the need of leaders and teachers which we reviewed earlier in the chapter. Except in the case of parents, the need has a different root. Divorced parents need this understanding because their personal feelings may tend to cloud their attitude toward the church and its teachings. While some may feel that they are not well-accepted, others may assume that the church condones their actions in particular and divorce in general and is not overly concerned about lifetime commitment in marriage. These faulty concepts need clarification if a divorced Christian is to deal realistically with his life experience in terms of its doctrinal and theological implications.

Possible Types of Training

In this section of the chapter we will look at some types of training which can assist divorced parents in rearing their children more happily and with better results. The format for the proposed content can take a variety of shapes. The most obvious format is a one-evening parent meeting designed specifically for divorced parents. In many congregations there is already a strong tradition of similar sessions for parents in general.

Some bodies of content can better be treated in a series of meetings with parents who are divorced. In such instances, the series may be conducted on consecutive days or evenings. Or it may be done in weekly or even monthly installments. If a church conducts seminars for divorced parents, much of the content needed can be incorporated into an already existing framework. In such cases, it may well be that a children's staff worker can be resource person for certain sessions while another church staff member carries the main responsibility for the seminar.

Retreat settings are also appropriate for any of the content we will be discussing. The more intense fellowship which is often developed in a retreat setting can enable divorced persons to open up to one another and to the retreat leader so that they deal with their problems at a deeper level than in other settings.

With these general observations about format in mind, let's take a closer look at possible content related to the needs which we have earlier listed.

Acceptance by others.—The body of content used in a seminar for divorced persons will not meet their deep needs for acceptance. For that, the "others" do have to accept the divorced person. But it is possible to help persons deal more effectively with their feelings of rejection. To do so, however, is considerably more difficult than to inform them of, say, the legal aspects of divorce. To attack the problem head-on, one must usually offer some sort of individual or group therapy.

In other words, this aspect of the divorced parent's need requires the services of a well-trained counselor. Such a person may be a member of the church staff. Or he may be a Christian whose full-time work is secular.

Self-understanding.—Once again we are dealing with a potentially sensitive issue. Genuine self-understanding is hard to come by. Most of us need expert help in achieving this level of insight.

However, some experiences can be provided. For instance, most denominational presses offer books and study units directly related to the development of self-understanding. These units are often accompanied by teaching guides or suggestions and other aids which a concerned lay person can use effectively.

None of this discussion is meant to minimize what can occur in the life of the person who participates regularly in Bible study and worship. One of the best things which a church staff member can do for divorced persons is to see that good provision is made for them in Sunday School and other Bible study settings and then to work diligently to involve them in Bible study.

Clarification of personal situations.—The first step here is to define the aspects of the personal situations which need clarification. With this understanding the content needed can be determined. For instance, if divorced persons lack understanding of the legal aspects of their divorce, they need both information and counseling. The general information which they need can be provided in a group setting with a competent lawyer as a resource person. Even if he or she cannot deal with each participant's questions in detail, he can at least help each parent formulate the questions he or she needs to ask his own lawyer.

A congregation or a group of congregations may also provide free legal advice to divorced parents who need it. At least these persons can be referred to community agencies which can provide such advice and assistance. The role of the staff worker with children may merely be to stimulate the interest of others in providing such direction.

Understanding their children.—Two bodies of content are clearly indicated in meeting this need. First of all, the divorced parent probably needs to broaden his understanding of childhood in general. Your denomination doubtless publishes material designed to help persons develop this kind of understanding. These materials can form the content for a child-study group composed of divorced parents.

A second body of content deals with the child of divorce. The material in the appendix to this book is a good resource for helping divorced parents develop understanding of the child of divorce. Using it this way requires some adaptation since the suggestions are designed for use with the children themselves.

In many congregations the best teacher or leader for either the general study or the specific study will likely be the staff worker with responsibility for children. In addition, many congregations include competent professionals in the area of child development or child guidance who can lead such study groups effectively.

Another sort of service which the professional children's worker can provide is not nearly so dramatic. The staff member can work behind the scenes to encourage divorced parents to participate in all general parent meetings. Remember that being obvious in recruiting divorced parents is tactless and may tend to say that the staff member considers these parents inherently unskilled and inferior in parenting.

Goals for the future.—The development of goals, since they are by nature specific to the person, may best be done in counseling one-to-one. Such counseling is probably the work of some staff member other than the children's worker. The person responsible for work with adults is probably the one who should arrange, if not conduct, group sessions related to goal-setting for divorced parents.

Bible teaching and church stance on divorce.—The content described in relation to helping leaders and teachers of children is equally applicable to divorced parents. And the same suggestions about leaders for such training also apply. Whether divorced parents and children's leaders would profit from a joint study depends upon the specific situation. That determination should be made by the church staff. Because of the potential sensitivity of the issue, divorced parents might be better served by studying as a separate group in which they feel freer to express their emotional reactions to the information they receive.

Helping Children of Divorce

We will deal only briefly with the needs of children which can be met by a church staff member. If you have already read chapter 2, you are aware of the needs of such children. Nor will we spend a great deal of time exploring ways in which they may be helped in groups through direct intervention. The appendix to this book provides the assistance a church staff member needs at that point.

Needs of Children of Divorce

Acceptance.—Like their troubled parents, the children of divorce may be struggling with an assortment of negative feelings about themselves. To experience unconditional acceptance by even a few significant others can make a world of difference in how well they cope with their problems.

Understanding basic aspects of divorce.—Many terms which adults readily understand are confusing to young children—even to older children. For instance, *alimony* is not a word which is used in day-by-day conversation. Children may even have been present in a courtroom when *custody* was awarded to the parent with whom they live and yet not understand the term itself. *Child support payments, visitation rights,* even *lawyer,*—the list goes on and on.

In addition many children simply do not understand the essential nature of the experience through which they are passing. They cannot identify the feelings which they sense between their parents, though they are deeply conscious of the tensions.

Understanding of their own emotions.—Being able to name a thing nearly always helps one deal with it. As far as many children can go in identifying their own feelings is to know that they feel bad. They cannot even distinguish between feeling bad "inside" and feeling bad physically. Knowing that the feelings one once could not name are perfectly legitimate is a wonderful relief to many children. Reassurance that eventually a person does recover good feelings about himself and, as a rule, about his parents is important.

Acceptance that divorce is final.—Even divorced persons themselves have difficulty accepting the fact that their broken marriage is not going to be restored. Children usually have even greater difficulty at this point. Yet to be able to recover their emotional equilibrium, they need to come to this recognition.

Possible Types of Training

Some group experience can be provided which can help children better cope with their situation. Experiences of this sort which we have found useful are a part of the content of the appendix.

We cannot emphasize too strongly the importance of face-to-face support for children of divorce. The learning experiences which we have suggested for workers and parents should help them provide some of this personal support. Church staff members, too, have this responsibility.

Setting for Group Experiences

The materials in the appendix are designed for five sessions of approximately two hours each. These sessions can be conducted on a variety of schedules. One session per week for five weeks is one pattern. In certain circumstances these sessions might be conducted independently of other meetings. In many instances, they will fit best into a schedule which includes parallel sessions for parents of the children in the group.

Regardless of the setting in which group experiences are provided, the leader for the sessions must be a competent and trained person. The obvious person in most congregations is the church staff member who has responsibility for children's work—if the church has such a staff member. In other congregations there are often persons who have professional training with children and who can provide such experiences in a mature way. At all costs, leadership for the group must not be surrendered to someone who is eager to help because "I feel so sorry for the sweet things, all torn up like that."

The leader must also be a person who is able to keep a secret. The leader is likely to hear things which should not become public property. Some observations which children make do not need to be shared with anyone, not even their parents. The leader must treat the sessions with the same degree of confidentiality which he expects from his own pastor, lawyer, and doctor. The same is true of information shared by parents in their individual or group meetings.

Community Resources

At several other points in the book we refer to community resources. Our intent in this section is to call your attention to some community resources which can relieve the problems of divorced parents and their children. No reference is intended as a blanket endorsement of a local agency. Before any of the resources cited in this chapter are used, that organization or agency should be checked.

Why list resources? A person is often unaware of the resources in a community until he or she has need of the services they provide. Thus, it is common to find people who are well-informed on world affairs and national concerns, yet who do not know what health, education, or human services are offered in their own communities. For this reason, we are suggesting a variety of resources which are available in most communities.

To whom does one turn for immediate help in solving problems which may seem overwhelming? Many studies, as well as the clinical experience of persons in the helping professions, indicate that a minister is the first person many people turn to for help. If you have a minister to whom troubled persons can go, we strongly recommend that you refer them to him. Some people turn to other family members. However, since you are dealing with a personal family problem, you may not feel that this source of help is desirable or indicated. Even when those close to a divorced person are able to be of some help, the person may need specific assistance beyond their capabilities to provide. The list of specific services and agencies, then, may provide the information you need.

We have included these resources for the following reasons:

Accessibility
Demonstrated record of service
Competency of staff
Economic feasibility
Appropriateness of agency.

Chamber of Commerce

The Chamber of Commerce in any city is concerned with the economic, social progress, and well-being of the community. This organization will help to plan and implement projects affecting the general welfare of a community. Therefore, Chambers of Commerce cooperate with government, business, and professional organizations in the community. Thus, the Chamber of Commerce is in an excellent position to know the economic and social needs of a community, and the resources to meet those needs.

Legal Services

Many larger cities have some kind of legal services agency which assists individuals and families with free legal assistance. These agencies will even represent persons unable to afford private attorneys in civil matters. For those who qualify for their services, a legal services agency will provide help with legal problems involving bills, loan companies, garnishments, landlords, child support, welfare eligibility, food stamps, Social Security, juvenile court cases, and other kinds of legal problems.

Homemakers Back to Work

Some communities with the aid of state funding provide job placement services specifically for divorced or widowed persons. Their goal is to place such persons back in the job market after an absence. Such an agency will assist a person in finding full- as well as part-time employment. Counseling and on-the-job training are also provided.

Parents Without Partners

Parents Without Partners is a national organization which has chapters in many communities. The organization is funded by nominal membership dues. It is a nonprofit, nonsectarian, educational organization devoted to the welfare and interests of single parents and their children.

Family and Children's Service

Most major cities have a Family and Children's Service agency. The primary purpose of this agency is to provide family and individual counseling. Their professionally trained staff provide services directed toward problems resulting in family crisis, disturbed family relationships, and personal adjustment of adults to children. Fees are on a sliding scale, based on ability to pay.

Boys' Club, Inc.

If a community has a boys' club, it will usually be affiliated with Boys' Clubs of America. This organization promotes the health, social, education, vocation, character and leadership development of boys. Their programs are usually building centered and professionally staffed.

Big Brothers/Big Sisters of America

Local agencies of this organization are composed primarily of volunteer laymen. The organization provides a child from a single parent home with an adult friend who can give regular guidance, understanding, and acceptance. A "match" is made with the assistance of a professionally trained social worker who also supervises and supports the relationship.

Boy Scouts of America

Scouting is an educational program for the character development, citizenship training, and mental and physical fitness of boys. The program is carried out locally through packs, troops, and explorer units. Scouting is conducted by adult leaders and volunteer workers, both men and women.

A comparable organization is available to girls through local groups known as Brownie Girl Scouts (age 6-8); Junior Girl Scouts (9-11); and Cadette Girl Scouts (12-14).

State Agencies

A variety of health, education, and human services are available through various state agencies in most communities. If you live in a rural area, information about these services may be obtained from county court offices. State agencies provide information about many private programs and services as well, since they often have planning and/or licensing responsibilities for such programs.

What Does This Mean for Me?

In this chapter we have given ideas which a children's worker on a church staff can shape to a program designed to help children of divorce in his or her own church. We suggest the following checklist for a professional church staff member with responsibility for children.

_____ 1. I have reviewed the needs of each category of persons described in this chapter, marking those which especially apply to the workers, parents, and children with whom I am personally acquainted.

_____ 2. I have reviewed the training suggestions made in relation to the needs I checked.

_____ 3. I have listed the training opportunities I can develop for use in my church.

_____ 4. I have ranked these possibilities in the order of priority.

_____ 5. I have developed a sequence for the events which will heighten their effectiveness.

_____ 6. I have prepared a tentative calendar for these events.

_____ 7. I have listed the persons within my church and community who could lead effectively in these events.

What you now have is the embryo of a plan for providing much needed assistance to children of divorce and to their families. Share this plan with the key people in the congregation who can help to shape it and to make it a reality. In most instances, you will first share the plan with the church staff, indicating the points at which you particularly need their help. Once the church staff has agreed upon a sound plan about which they are enthusiastic, share it with the other persons in the church whose cooperation will be essential to success.

Then carry out your plan!

Reading for Enrichment

All the books on this list will be useful for the children's worker on a church staff, although the categories listed here are limited. The inclusion of a book on this list is not an endorsement of all the views expressed in that book. Books, especially those for children, should be reviewed by the person responsible for their use before they are made available to children or to others.

General

Is There a Family in the House, Kenneth Chafin. Word Books, 1978. Chapter 9,

"Healing Broken Relationships," and chapter 10, "Allies for the Family," dealing with divorce.

The Games Children Play, A. H. Chapman. G. P. Putnam, 1972. Discusses emotional strategies children use on one another, on their parents, and on other adults.

When Families Hurt, W. Douglas Cole. Broadman Press, 1979. Deals with a wide variety of family problems, including divorce. No single problem is given in-depth treatment, but the material is a starting point.

Hide or Seek, James Dobson. Revell Company, 1974. Deals with basic feelings of children and their expression, giving ten strategies for helping children develop good self-images.

Children of Divorce, J. Louis Despert. Doubleday & Co., 1953, 1972. Gives insights and suggestions for handling children's adjustment to divorce.

How to Father, Fitzhugh Dobson. Nash Publishing, 1974. Offers a practical guide for fathers covering all the stages of child development from birth to age twenty-one.

How to Parent, Fitzhugh Dobson. Nash Publishing, 1970. Describes the daily development of children, starting from infancy, and the role of the mother in building a positive self-concept for herself and her children.

Counseling for Church Leaders, John Drakeford. Broadman Press, 1961. Offers basic techniques for the church counselor and includes one chapter on marriage counseling.

Evelyn Duvall's Handbook for Parents, Evelyn Mills Duvall. Broadman Press, 1974. Traces the development of children through infancy and early childhood to the teens with practical advice for parents.

Between Parent and Child: New Solutions to Old Problems. Haim G. Ginott. Macmillan Co., 1965. Presents a conversational how-to approach to communicating with children.

Parent Effectiveness Training, Thomas Gordon. Wyden Co., 1970. Uses dozens of lively case histories; shows step-by-step how a democratic method enlists youngsters to participate in dealing with conflicts.

Discipline in the Christian Home, Wayne W. Grant. Convention Press, 1975. Consists of four chapters: I. Discipline: What Is It?; II. Where It All Begins; III. Methods of Discipline; and IV. Practical Situations in Discipline. The last part of the book consists of suggested learning activities.

Growing Parents, Growing Children, Wayne W. Grant. Convention Press, 1977. Offers information parents need to know about children from birth to the teen years. The book is easy to read.

Divorced Parents

An Open Book to the Christian Divorcee, Roger H. Crook. Broadman Press, 1974. Explores courses of action for the divorced Christian without attempting to justify or condemn divorce. Includes chapters on religion, children, and law.

Explaining Divorce to Children, Earl A. Grollman. Consists of ten chapters, each by a different person. The book offers practical suggestions for explaining divorce to children and for helping them make a satisfactory adjustment to divorce.

Talking About Divorce, Earl A. Grollman. Beacon Press, 1975. Provides a child-level picture book for a divorced parent to use with his or her child. Special section tells the parent how to use the book.

Coping with Being Single Again, Clark Hensley. Broadman Press, 1978. Deals in reasonable depth with problems faced by both widowed and divorced persons, offering guidance for resolving problems.

Working Mothers, Lois W. Hoffman and F. Ivan Nye. Jossey Bass Publishers, 1974. Presents research findings concerning the motivations and consequences of women entering the labor force.

Bachelor Fatherhood, Michael McFadden. Walker & Co., 1974. Offers practical advice about divorce, raising children, running a household, cooking, and readjusting to life as a bachelor.

The Divorcee's Handbook, Louise Rohner. Doubleday, 1967 (paperback by Bantam Press). Chapter 5, "Bless the Children," and chapter 10, "Mama's Boyfriend," include some helpful pointers on handling the everyday aspects of single motherhood.

Helps for the Single-Parent Christian Family, Charles E. Smith. Convention Press, 1978. Gives the divorced or widowed parent help in healthy acceptance of himself and his situation plus practical guidelines for parenting alone.

When Parents Divorce, Bernard Steinzor. Pantheon Books, 1969. Another approach to divorce which you may find refreshing. Relationships between children and parents after divorce are discussed.

Children

I Have Feelings, Terry Berger. Behavioral Publications, 1971. Covers seventeen different feelings, both good and bad, and the situations that precipitate each one.

The Boys and Girls Book About Divorce, Richard A. Gardner. Bantam Press, 1970. A book written for children, fifth grade through junior high school.

Where Is Daddy? the Story of a Divorce, Beth Goff. Beacon Press, 1969. Feelings like fear, anger, and sadness which accompany divorce are sensitively dealt with in the award-winning book.

Emily and the Klunky Baby and the Next Door Dog, Joan M. Lexau. Dial Press,

1972. Angry with her divorced mother, Emily decides to run away with the baby to live with Daddy.

Me Day, Joan M. Lexau. Dial Press, 1971. A book about a child's reaction to divorce and how delicate the celebration of a special day can be in a single-parent home.

My Daddy Lives in a Downtown Hotel, Peggy Mann. Doubleday, 1973. A young boy tries to adapt to his parent's pending divorce and the changes it will make in his life.

Morris and His Brave Lion, Helen S. Rogers. McGraw-Hill, 1975. One day Morris meets his first lion, and the next he hears the word *divorce.* Morris uses the lion to help bring his father back to see him again.

A Father Like That, Charlotte Zolotow. Harper & Row, 1971. This book is about a boy who tries to imagine what his father would be like.

David Asks, "Why?", Linda S. Chandler. Broadman Press, 1981. David's questions and feelings about his parent's divorce will help boys and girls and parents talk about divorce.

Appendix: Resources

To Use This Appendix You Need to Know . . .

The Purpose of the Appendix

This appendix offers suggestions for a seminar for children in grades three through six whose parents are divorced or are in the process of divorcing. It is intended for use by church staff members or other professionals related to children of this age.

The Nature of the Seminar Experience

In conducting the seminar, you are embarking upon an adventure different from the adventure in most other teaching in church settings. This is true because of the relationship you will have to the participants. You are about to discover a new dimension in surrogate parenting. One can readily see why this should be so. The children with whom you will deal are all children who have only one parent in the home. This fact in itself means that some of them will, consciously or unconsciously, be seeking a substitute parent.

Another unique dimension of the experience is its intensity. Because you will deal with one of the biggest single events in the lives of the boys and girls in the group, tension may often run high.

A third distinctive of this experience is that it does not go in a straight line. You are likely to find yourself dealing with nearly any of the seminar content in almost any session simply because the children push you that way. In many teaching situations, the emphasis is on imparting and acquiring information. The primary content in this course is feelings. And feelings depend upon—well, upon feelings rather than reason. Expect to move back and forth from feeling to feeling as well as to share information.

Who Are the Learners?

In response to the question, let us share some things we learned through experience. First, restrict the learners to children who are in the third to sixth grades. We've tried the seminar with children younger than third grade and must admit that we helped them less than we had hoped to. Younger children generally lack the social and emotional maturity necessary to deal with the divorce experience in such a setting.

Second, limit the number to about ten, or at the most twelve, boys and girls. Once we tried to accommodate a larger group simply because so many parents wanted their children to participate. But you will be operating at a level which requires a low pupil-teacher ratio.

Third, insist on a parental commitment for 100 percent attendance on the part of any child enrolled. Since the suggested learning activities interlock, making up a missed session is impossible.

Securing this commitment may be tied to preregistration procedures. A brochure explaining the content of the course, the necessity of commitment on the part of the parent, and blanks supplying basic information about the child is advisable. Basic information includes at least name, address, telephone number, school grade, age, parent who has custody, and how long the parent has been divorced. Other information may be desired by a particular leader.

Fourth, you may need contact with families during the course of the seminar. We discovered in one instance that the course was proving more traumatic for a child than we suspected from his conduct in the group. Had we known that fact earlier, we would have suggested that he drop out.

What About the Teacher?

That question may seem a bit daft in view of the fact that you are likely a professional children's worker. But we feel honor bound to call some factors to your attention. The teacher should be a person who

Has a solid professional background in childhood education, preferably both in secular and religious education.

Has worked closely with children and enjoys them.

Is seriously concerned about helping children of divorce.

Is eager to plan carefully and to redesign plans to meet the needs of children.

Can accept negative emotion and tension without going to pieces.

Knows how to keep a confidence as must any professional who counsels others.

We have only one more caution: Don't attempt the class alone. We didn't, and we wouldn't. You need a companion in this high adventure. Select someone with whom you are compatible and who already has your respect as a professional and as a Christian.

What About Preparation?

Before you settle down to preparing for the seminar itself, read every word of the book. You will inevitably read it from the viewpoint of a professional children's worker. Try also to study the individual chapters through the eyes of other potential readers: parents, lay leaders, or persons who are merely curious.

Examine your motives for conducting the seminar. The seminar is not the sort of experience to enter halfheartedly because someone else thinks providing it would be a nice thing to do.

Read all of the appendix carefully. Evaluate the suggestions in terms of the boys and girls you anticipate having in your group.

Adapt the suggestions to better meet the needs of the children you will teach. Then as each session is completed, you can adapt what you have planned for following sessions. In this way the course becomes better with each session.

Check resources before you complete planning. Be sure all teaching aids are ready and that you know how to use them. Survey all other resources needed. (We have tried to keep these suggestions to a minimum except for items such as pencils and paper.)

What Sort of a Physical Setting Is Best?

You probably have a choice of several meeting places. Select the one which provides the most comfortable setting. Avoid a room so large that it invites excessive movement. And avoid one in which boys and girls—and the teaching team—will feel penned in when emotions run high.

Obviously you need a room which provides tables and chairs. We have tried not to suggest activities which require a great deal of other equipment.

One other thing: If you follow through on the suggestions for outdoor activities, you need a room with easy access to a play area. Having to go long distances through corridors and up or down stairs is an open invitation to rowdiness.

What About the Schedule?

We project five sessions of approximately two hours each, though this schedule can be altered to fit your needs. Boys and girls need a break in so long a session, so we suggest a mid-session time-out of about twenty minutes with refreshments.

In relationship to each activity we are also noting a time estimate. These estimates are based on our experiences, and we hope they will be helpful to you.

What Behaviors Can Teachers Expect?

What you know about the boys and girls who will be in your class and their general conduct from other experiences with them is the best basis for an answer to the question. It does, however, seem to us that boys and girls in this setting tend to be a bit more extreme in their behavior than others. For instance, both rowdiness and withdrawal may be more evident than in a randomly selected group of children. Another thing you need to know is that many children of divorce compensate for their difficulties by eating. You may or may not find obese children in the group. The groups we have taught put away an uncommon amount of punch and cookies.

What Do Children Have at the End of the Seminar?

In the course of the sessions, boys and girls will accumulate a number of materials. Most of these will be items they personally develop. These items are described fully in the procedures suggested in the appendix. Models for some items are also included.

We suggest that a file folder be prepared for each child. Session by session the materials he completes can be stored in his folder. It is important that the folders be left in the care of the leader. At the completion of the course, the materials can be incorporated into a notebook. Instructions for preparing covers for notebooks are included in this appendix.

The purpose of the notebook is, of course, to give each child something he can keep after the course is over. The content will remind him of his seminar experiences and can reinforce what he learns which is of lasting value to him. The notebook also becomes something to be shared with a parent, opening avenues to better understanding between parent and child.

What About Sessions with Parents?

We have found a follow-up session with parents helpful to us and to them. Each time we have conducted the seminar we have done so in connection with a seminar for parents. So the parents of the children with whom we dealt were involved in an experience roughly similar to that of their children.

In these sessions we shared the general things which we felt would be helpful to parents. We carefully refrained from betraying the confidence of any child. And we invited parents' questions, answering as honestly and as openly as we knew how. You will probably wish to correlate the content of your sessions with any content used in the parent seminar if the two are conducted simultaneously.

What you want to do about parent counseling beyond one session is up to you. You alone know your limitations. For ourselves, we like to leave the door open for the parent who wishes to approach us privately, though we have not wished to become involved in a full-scale program of parent counseling.

Congratulations on the adventure you are about to have. May you find the experience as rewarding as we have.

Session 1

To Get Ready

As you complete each action on this list, place a check in the blank preceding it.

_____Read the suggested procedure, evaluating each activity in terms of your group.

_____Prepare items 1, 2, 3, and 4 described later in this appendix.

_____Secure pencils, at least one marking pencil, a variety of crayons or felt-tipped markers, construction paper in several colors, masking tape, file folders, and Bibles.

_____If possible, secure a picture of Samuel as a young child.

_____Review the story of Timothy and secure an appropriate picture of Timothy.

_____Prepare the sentence-strip titles for activities as described in the procedures.

_____Arrange for light refreshments.

_____Set up the room for maximum comfort and convenience, providing at-table seating for all.

_____Pray for the children and for yourself and for the person(s) with whom you will be teaching.

Leading the Session

Making Name Tags (approximately 10 min.).—As children arrive, invite each to make a name tag, using the available materials to make whatever sort of tag he wishes. Workers should make tags, too. Talk informally with the boys and girls as they work, following their leads. Have each child attach his name tag to his clothing with a masking tape loop.

Playing Who Am I (approximately 20 min.).—Use the Who Am I? gameboard (item 1, page 141). Let the children take turns spinning the arrow. When the arrow stops, the child tells something about himself which relates to the subject indicated. Workers should participate also.

As an alternate way to play, a child who spins the arrow can ask any other child to tell about himself when the arrow stops. The child who responds can then spin the arrow. Be sure that every child is called on before any child is invited to respond the second time.

At the conclusion of the activity, guide children in recalling all they can about one another.

Sharing Booklet Plans (approximately 5 min.).—Explain to the children that at the end of the course each will have a booklet to help him recall what he has learned and to share with his family. Describe how the booklets will be put together and decorated.

Making Who Am I? Information Sheets (approximately 10 min.).—Distribute an information sheet (item 2, page 142) to each child. Explain that this sheet will be the first item in each person's booklet. Ask each child to complete the sheet as carefully as possible. Give assistance needed. When papers are completed, file them in folders. If a child finishes sooner than others, encourage him to decorate the page with pictures related to the information or with a border design.

Previewing the Sessions (approximately 10 min.).—Prepare a short statement to describe each major element you plan to include in the sessions. Keep statements brief.

Show the poster strips one by one. Discuss each statement, allowing children to ask questions. Then display the statements on a sentence strip chart or on a tackboard. This display can be used in later sessions as a reminder of the direction of the course.

Remind the children that some Bible people also lived with people other than their immediate families. Allow children to guess who these people might be. (Two whom the children may know are Timothy and Samuel.) If possible display pictures of Timothy and Samuel and encourage conversation about these Bible boys. (Note: See Acts 16:1-2; 2 Tim. 1:1-5; and 1 Sam. 1:9-13, 20-28.)

Taking a Break (approximately 20 min.).—If possible, arrange for the break away from the meeting room. Children might be allowed ten minutes on an adjacent playground. Serve refreshments at the end of the break, rather than at the beginning, to encourage children to return to the session more readily.

Sharing a Story About Timothy (approximately 15 min.).—Call attention to a picture of Timothy. Then tell the story, adapting it as necessary to better fit the level of the group.

Timothy

Timothy grew up in the city of Lystra. The Bible does not tell us about Timothy's father. We do know that Timothy lived with his mother, Eunice, and his grandmother Lois.

When he was growing up, Timothy learned about the great heroes told about in the Old Testament. His mother and grandmother told him about men like Moses and David and about women like Ruth and Deborah. Eunice and Lois helped Timothy understand what God expects of each person.

When the great Christian missionary Paul came to Lystra, Timothy listened to what Paul told about Jesus. He thought about Paul's words, and he used what he had learned to test the truth of what Paul said. Timothy knew that God would send a Savior. And he believed with all his heart that Jesus was that Savior.

The next time Paul came to Lystra, he was in need of a young man to help him with the work of telling people everywhere about Jesus. How delighted Paul was to know that all the Christians in Lystra had a good opinion of Timothy. Paul knew that Timothy would be just the person he needed to help him.

Timothy traveled with Paul for a long time. Later he was a leader in one of the churches which Paul started. When Paul was far away from Timothy, he wrote a letter to Timothy. He called Timothy a term which must have made Timothy happy.

—based on Acts

At this point have the children find the term Paul called Timothy: "my own son in the faith" (1 Tim. 1:2).

Conclude the activity with conversation, emphasizing the fact that Timothy may not have had a live-in father during much of his life. If it seems appropriate, emphasize that sometimes others are like family members to a child who lives in a one-parent family.

Introducing Terms Related to Divorce (approximately 40 min.).—Distribute copies of the puzzle (item 4, page 143) and pencils. Challenge each child to work on his own. Provide assistance when a child becomes stuck. Encourage children to ask questions and to share ideas about the terms. Avoid letting the activity become too competitive, either in terms of speed or performance.

When the children have finished, file each child's puzzle in his folder.

Guide the children in entering the words on the Wall Puzzle. (See item 3, page 143.) Read a definition and let a volunteer place that word on the puzzle with the marking pencil. Continue to encourage the children to ask questions and to discuss the meaning of the words.

At the end of the session, tell the children what they can expect in the next session. Be enthusiastic so they will look forward to the session.

After the session, take a few minutes to review what has been done in the session. With your fellow worker(s) determine what could be done to make the next session even better.

Session 2

To Get Ready

Check the blank for each of the preparation steps as you complete them.

_____Study carefully all of the procedures for this session.

_____Review each of the "Who Am I?" sheets the children completed during the previous session.

_____Prepare items 5, 6, and 7.

_____Collect scissors, masking tape, and string. Also have enough 8½ by 11" sheets of papers, pencils, and/or crayons for the children who may choose to draw pictures of their homes.

Leading the Session

Greeting the Children (approximately 5 min.).—Try to call each child by name as he arrives. Use the name tags made in the first session, or let children make new ones.

Play "Flash Card Game" (approximately 15 min.).—Mount on the wall or a bulletin board the crossword wall puzzle used in the first session. If the puzzle was covered with self-adhesive transparency, clean it. (If you did not cover the puzzle for reuse, draw it on a chalkboard or make a new copy for this session.)

Show the picture on one of the flash cards. Let children try to recall the word or term used for this picture in the puzzle. When the correct word is identified, show the children the word on the back of the picture. Then allow the child who correctly identified the picture to come to the board and write the word in the puzzle.

Continue until all the words have been identified and the puzzle is completed. Do not rush discussion of terms.

Introduce "How Divorce Changed Things for Them" (approximately 40 min.).—Explain to the children that they have the opportunity to be in a sort of play and that each person who takes a part will get to use a face mask. (See item 7, page 146.) Allow volunteers to choose the masks they wish to use.

Distribute the "Role Play Cards" (item 6, page 145) according to the masks the children have chosen. Ask each child to read his card carefully to become familiar with the words of the character he is to play. Encourage the children to read the statements with feeling and to feel free to put their character's comments into their own words.

You may wish to repeat the role play, giving other children a chance to participate. Or you may wish to give a child an opportunity to play a different part.

Remind the children that the reactions of the children in the role play are the most common reactions of children to divorce. Allow opportunity, but do not force any child to say that he has had or does have one or more of the feelings expressed by the role-play children.

After the children have completed the role play, announce that another game making use of the masks will be played immediately after the break. Collect the masks and role-play cards and allow the children to begin the break.

Taking a Break (approximately 20 min.).—While one leader supervises the free play or games with the children, another can prepare the room for the second session. If you choose to have refreshments, serve them as soon as the children return to the room. During the break, attach the face masks to a wall or bulletin board.

Use the Role-Play Cards (approximately 10 min.).—Distribute a role-play card to each person, being sure that each gets a card he has not used before. Let the children take turns reading the cards. As each child reads his card, the other children will look at the displayed masks and try to match the comments with the appropriate mask.

If you prefer to use it, here is a variation. Let the leader(s) read the cards. The children can take turns being first to match comments with a mask.

Deal with the Question: How Has Divorce Changed Things for You?.—All of the activities of this session have pointed toward this discussion. It is important for children to express their feelings, but none should be forced to do so. The leader should stay in charge of the discussion so that each child who wishes to express his thoughts can be heard in an atmosphere of acceptance and understanding. Each child should understand that the leader will hold in strict confidence any personal information the child feels like sharing.

Open the way for discussion by saying something like this: "Each of the children we've pretended to be felt differently about his parents' divorce. But for each one things did seem to change after the divorce. I'm wondering if any of you feels that things in your life have been changed by your parents' divorce. Would you like to tell us how things have changed for you?"

An alternate activity for the children who do not wish to take part in the discussion is to draw pictures of their homes. One leader should work closely with any child who chooses to draw a picture. His comments can easily open the way for the same freedom of discussion that lets the child talk about his feelings.

Close with Prayer (approximately 5 min.).—In your prayer express appreciation for each one who is present and for the fact that God helps us in all problems.

As the children leave, encourage them to be present for the next session. Giving them a hint about what will take place may help.

When the children are gone, take a few minutes to review plans for the next session. What changes, if any, need to be made in the light of what has taken place in this session? Can the room be made more attractive or more comfortable? Does some child need an extra measure of attention?

Session 3

To Get Ready

Place a check in the appropriate blank as you complete each action.

_____Study the procedural suggestions to determine their value in meeting the needs of your boys and girls.

_____Review your plans for the session, adapting them as advisable.

_____Prepare items 6, 8, 9, 10, and 11.

_____Secure other materials needed for activities.

_____Pray for the boys and girls, for their families, for yourself, and for the session.

Leading the Session

Identify Feelings (approximately 10 min.).—Place the "They Felt This Way" strips (item 8, page 147) on a table or floor in view of the children. Explain that you will review the role plays used in the previous session. Children will look at the strips as each story is told. They will select the strip which best describes the feeling experienced by the story child. Continue until all the stories are used.

Encourage the children to discuss the reasons for their choices. As terms are selected, children can place them on a sentence strip board. Or the strips may be taped or tacked on a display wall.

Children are likely to select at least one strip which does not best describe a story child's feeling. Permit them to place the strip on display anyway.

When all strips are in place, guide the children in reevaluating all choices. Explain that not every child whose parents divorce experiences all of the feelings but that many children experience all of the feelings at one time or another.

Distribute the "They Felt This Way" matching charts (item 9, page 147), one for each child. Let the children draw lines connecting the names of the story children and their feelings. Collect the sheets and file them in the proper folders for inclusion in notebooks.

Claim Personal Feelings (approximately 25 min.).—Ask the children to assist in placing the "They Felt This Way" strips at different places about the room. Instruct them that you will play a recording. While the music is playing, they are to find and stand by the strip which describes their present feeling about the divorce in their family. Play a brief excerpt from the recording.

Then call attention to how many of the children found a statement which describes their present feelings. If any child wishes to talk about his feelings, permit him to do so. Avoid forcing a child to comment, and discourage the kind of sharing you suspect a child may later regret doing. If a child does not wish to stand by any strip, assure him that this is an OK action.

Explain that when the music plays again, each child is to stand by another strip which describes a feeling he has often had. Let children discuss their choices. Repeat the same procedure as many times as seems productive.

At the conclusion of the activity, comment that each feeling is normal and natural. Emphasize that learning to deal with feelings is important and that during the seminar the children will get help in doing so.

Express Feelings Through Writing or Art (approximately 20 min.).—Explain that each child can either write about his experiences and feelings or he can use the materials to create a picture representing his feelings. Indicate that there is no one right way to perform this activity, but that each child's creation will be precisely right for him.

If the activity is too threatening for a child, let him help straighten the room or check folder contents to be sure materials are correctly filed. Help this child understand that failure to produce an essay or picture is acceptable behavior.

During the time children are working, encourage them to talk about what they are doing and the feelings they have. Help in any way the children indicate they need assistance. Avoid, however, making a picture or writing a description for a child. The finished product is far less important than the process involved. At the conclusion of the activity, place the products in the proper file folders.

Taking a Break (approximately 20 min.).—Follow basically the same procedure which you have used in previous sessions. Remember that serving refreshments at the conclusion of the free time encourages children to return promptly.

Deal with Your Feelings (approximately 20 min.).—Let the children group themselves on the floor around teachers. Teachers may then take turns reading the open-end stories (page 148). Children may work together to develop endings, or they may take turns as individuals.

If children are regular churchgoers, they may have learned to complete open-end stories patly. Challenge them to tell how the stories would end in most families, not the way they think the stories ought to end. Use discretion in guiding the group in evaluating the endings they suggest.

Discuss with children how they think each child in the stories felt about himself if he or she behaved as suggested. Guide children in considering what next steps the story child might take. If children wish to do so, let them suggest alternate endings for any story.

Find Bible Verses to Help (approximately 20 min.).—Ask boys and girls to share ideas about ways to cope with the conduct they described in completing the open-end stories. If they do not make the suggestion, call their attention to the fact that Bible verses can help people understand how to handle tough situations.

Distribute copies of item 11 (page 151). Instruct boys and girls to select the verse or verses which they feel would help a boy or girl in the situations described on the sheet.

Remember that the activity is not a test. Encourage discussion of the verses in light of the situations. If a child selects a verse that seems inappropriate, encourage him to reevaluate his choice, but avoid implying that he has made a dumb choice.

To conclude the activity, encourage each boy and girl to select one verse which he believes will be helpful to him personally. Then lead each pupil to memorize his verse. As time permits, children can say their verses to the group and explain why they chose these verses.

Conclude the Session (approximately 5 min.).—Lead boys and girls in prayer, expressing appreciation for the time together and for being able to share important experiences.

After the session, straighten the room, leaving it in good order. As you do so, go over the events in the session. Consider the degree to which each activity met its intended purpose. Determine changes needed in plans for session 4.

Session 4

To Get Ready

As you complete each action, place a check in the appropriate blank.

_____Study all suggestions and determine which can best meet the needs of your boys and girls.

____Prepare items 12 and 13.

____Make arrangements for the break.

____Gather other materials needed for the activities you choose to use.

Leading the Session

Complete Creative Writing or Drawing (approximately 20 min.).—Allow time for any child who may not have completed this activity during the previous session to do so now. Be alert for clues to feelings which children reveal by their offhand remarks as they complete their work.

Share Work from Previous Session (approximately 20 min.).—Let the children show items from their files. As they share their work and discuss their feelings, try to affirm that things are changing for everyone all the time. Even in homes without divorce, many parents and children experience some of the same changes that children from homes of divorce experience. Any child is likely to have to move to a new residence. Some children have to live with only one parent, or with grandparents, because of the death of one parent. Talk about these facts with the children, emphasizing that the longer one lives the more likely he is to face changes of one kind or another in his life.

Use the "How Divorce Sometimes Changes Things" Wall Chart (approximately 10 min.).—Since you will have just discussed the fact that things are changing for everybody, it should be easy to make the transition to using the wall chart. After attaching the chart to the board or wall, read all of it with the children. Allow them to respond orally to each statement. Such group participation should help each child respond more freely.

Try to help each person to see some similarities in his experiences and the experiences of other members of the group. This in itself is a helpful exercise for the children. There is a certain amount of reassurance in knowing that others have problems similar to your own. On the other hand, this activity can also help the children to see that each person's life situation is a little different from every other person's.

Taking a Break (approximately 20 min.).—By this time the children should be familiar with the break routine. They know that refreshments will be ready when they return to the room.

Complete "How Divorce Changed Things for Me" Work Sheets (approximately 20 min.).—Each child should complete a copy of the "How Divorce Changed Things for Me" work sheet (item 13). While completing the work sheet, some of the children may need to talk about how divorce has changed things for them.

Catch Up on Activities (remainder of session).—Allow the children to do any activity they may have missed earlier or to complete work left unfinished. Explain that now is a good time for trying to get answers to any questions not yet answered. Or it may be a time for expressing any feelings or fears which one may have. Finally, it may be a time for completing notebook items.

Collect the children's booklets at the end of the session. Remind them that the next session will be the last one. Then close the session with prayer.

After the session, examine each child's booklet to determine the progress he or she has made. This review will help you know which children need special help during the next session. In addition to work not completed, also notice mistakes and misunderstandings the child may reveal. By noting these facts and calling upon your previous observations, you will be better prepared to help each child bring the study to a successful completion during the final session.

Session 5

To Get Ready

Place a check in each of the blanks as you complete the actions.

_____Study carefully all of the procedures for this session.

_____Prepare item 14.

_____Secure additional supplies and materials the children will need in order to complete their booklets.

_____Read the following story which is to be used during the first part of the period.

The setting for the story is England. The story is about a man whose name was Thomas Hobson, and he lived about four hundred years ago. Mr. Hobson lived many years before automobiles were invented. The best way to get from one place to another in those days was to ride a horse. Mr. Hobson owned many horses which he kept in a stable and rented to people who needed a horse to ride.

Mr. Hobson had a problem in that many people found it difficult to decide which horse they wanted to rent. Finally Mr. Hobson made a rule which everyone who wanted to rent a horse from him had to follow. His rule was this: If you want to rent a horse, you have to take the first horse in line, or you don't get a horse at all.

If a person did not like the first horse in line, his choice was between a horse he didn't like and no horse at all. This sort of choice soon came to be known as "Hobson's Choice."

This term has been handed down to us from generation to generation. So, today when a person is said to have a "Hobson's Choice," we mean that he must choose between something he doesn't like and nothing at all.

We have talked about the fact that mothers and fathers are sometimes so unhappy in their marriage that they must choose between a bad marriage and no marriage at all. When this happens, they have a "Hobson's Choice." Most parents want to choose what they believe will be best for their children. As unhappy as a child may be with his parents' decision, it is helpful to remember that the parents may have had a "Hobson's Choice."

_____Be prepared to give each child his booklet as he enters the room. Any child who arrives early may use the time before the session to work on his booklet.

Leading the Session

Tell the Story of Thomas Hobson (approximately 10 min.).—Either read the story of Thomas Hobson or tell it in your own words. You can make the story more exciting and fun by adding imaginary details about the kinds of nags which were first in line when prospective customers arrived at Mr. Hobson's stable. Describe how the customers felt when they had to take a nag although a good horse was next in line.

Discuss Application of the Story (approximately 10 min.).—Ask each child to think for a few minutes about the reasons why he believes his parents divorced. Encourage any who wish to do so to share what they think, but do not pry or probe. If no child seems inclined to talk at this point, you can suggest some major reasons why people divorce. Try to avoid statements which sound as if you are deliberately describing the family situation of any one of the children.

Then ask: "Would you say that reasons like these give parents a 'Hobson's Choice'?" Try to help children better understand the difficulty their parents faced in making their decision.

Draw a "Hobson's Choice" Picture (approximately 20 min.).—Provide essential materials for children to draw pictures to remind themselves of the meaning of "Hobson's Choice." Since the idea of drawing horses may dismay some children, be ready to suggest alternatives such as drawing pictures of the faces of people having to make such choices. Some children may prefer to write a slogan and decorate the margins of the page. When pictures are complete, add them to the appropriate file folders.

Take a Break (approximately 20 min.).—You may wish to provide some sort of extra for this final session—a few extra minutes of a favorite game, a special dessert for refreshments.

Decide "What I've Learned" (approximately 20 min.).—Display the strips you made for the first session telling what the content of the seminar would be. Let pupils recall something of what they learned about each area of content. Then ask this question: "What is the one thing you've learned or felt that you will remember the longest?'' After the boys and girls have had time to think of their answers, encourage those who wish to do so to share their answers. Then ask each person to write his or her answer on a sheet of notebook paper for inclusion in his book.

Assemble and Decorate Notebooks (approximately 30 min.).—Distribute to each person the papers he has completed as a part of the course. Also provide construction paper or tagboard for making notebook covers. Encourage boys and girls to individualize their notebooks with drawings and designs.

You may wish to suggest that the notebooks be assembled in the order in which the items were created. Doing so will give one more opportunity to recall the events of the course. Use tact and judgment in encouraging participants to recall emotional moments.

As the time draws to a close, talk with the boys and girls about how they will use their notebooks. Let them suggest uses. But be sure that these two uses are mentioned: (1) Share with parents and discuss what has been learned, and (2) Review from time to time to remember what was learned. Other uses might include sharing the notebook with some other child whose parents are divorcing or have recently divorced.

Evaluating the Course (approximately 10 min.).—Prepare an evaluation sheet for each pupil to complete. (Item 14, page 153) provides an example, but your evaluation sheet should be tailor-made for the sessions you have conducted.) Explain to the boys and girls that you need to know what they think about the course so that you can help other boys and girls in the future. Give them the option of signing their papers or leaving them unsigned. Answer questions about the evaluation sheets only for the purpose of clarification in order to avoid influencing the children's comments.

Closing the Seminar (approximately 5 min.).—You will need to develop an approach workable with your class. Here is one possibility. Have the group form a circle. Then go around the circle saying something helpful about each child. For instance: "I am glad Carl was in our group because he always helped straighten the room." Or: "I'm glad Betty was in the group because she shared her ideas so freely."

Then close the session with a prayer. Thank God for each boy and girl and for his or her home, asking God to help all in the room improve in their skills as family members.

After the session, review the evaluation sheets with your fellow worker(s). You may feel that a full analysis of the sheets should be reserved for a later time when more attention can be given to the matter. If so, set a definite time and place. And then when this session is held, write down the things you want to remember in planning and conducting a future seminar.

Item 1: "Who Am I?" Gameboard

Prepare a gameboard like the illustration, making it approximately 12″ in diameter. Attach a pointer at the center with a brad, being sure that the hole in the pointer is large enough to permit the pointer to spin freely.

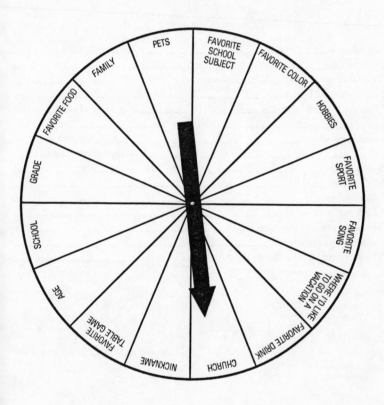

Item 2: "Who Am I?" Information Sheet

Prepare a copy of the following information sheet for each pupil. Be sure blanks are large enough for a child's writing. Allow additional lines as you see fit.

Who Am I?

My name is_____.

I live at_____in_____, _____.

The other people in my home include_____.

During school I attend_____.

I have completed the_____grade. My favorite subject is_____. My teacher is_____.

I attend church at_____where I am in the
_____Sunday School Department.

My eyes are_____, and my hair is_____.

My favorite food is_____.

I like to play_____.

My favorite animal is_____.

My best vacation was when_____.

I will always remember_____.

The most important thing about me is_____.

Item 3: Divorce Wall Puzzle

Print a copy of the puzzle in item 4 on poster board at least 17″ by 22″. Cover the puzzle with clear adhesive-backed plastic. Let children use a marking pencil when filling blanks in the puzzle.

Item 4: Divorce Crossword Puzzle

Make a master of the puzzle and clues given here. Prepare a copy for each pupil.

ACROSS

1. D _ _ _ _ _ _ _—A complete breaking of the marriage relation between husband and wife.

2. J _ _ _ _ _—A public officer who conducts or presides over a court of justice.

3. C _ _ _ _ S _ _ _ _ _ _ _—An allowance granted to a divorced wife (usually) for the maintenance of children placed in her care.
4. H _ _ _—The place where a family lives.
5. V _ _ _ _ _ _ _ _ R _ _ _ _ _ _—The right of a divorced parent who does not have custody of a minor child to visit the child at such times and places as the court may decide.
6. A _ _ _ _ _ _ _—An allowance for the support and care of one's divorced spouse.
7. F _ _ _ _ _ _—The persons who live in one house.

DOWN

1. C _ _ _ _ _—An organ of government, consisting of one or more persons, given the authority to administer justice.
2. L _ _ _ _ _ _—An attorney or counselor at law.
3. C _ _ _ _ _ _ _—The control and care of children.
4. S _ _ _ _ _ _ _ _ _ _—When husband and wife cease to live together with the intention of getting a divorce.
5. S _ _ _ _ _ _—A word used for husband or wife.
6. C _ _ _ _ _ H _ _ _ _ _ _ _—Presenting and considering proofs and arguments with respect to an issue.

Item 5: Flash Cards

Place each term from item 4 on a 4″ x 6″ card. On the back of each card paste a picture suggesting the term. Here are suggestions.

TERM	PICTURE
Divorce	Angry looking man and woman standing back to back or walking away from one another
Judge	Judge (male or female) presiding from podium
Child support	Check or currency and a child
Home	House with family in yard
Alimony	Check or currency and a woman with at least one child
Family	A group of people eating at a kitchen table
Court	Courtroom, possibly empty
Lawyer	Lawyer questioning person on stand
Custody	Mother or father watching over children at play
Separation	Two houses, one with a man beside it and the other with a woman beside it
Court hearing	Two lawyers standing before judge
Spouse	Two pictures, a man and a woman
Visiting rights	Children running from a house toward a waiting car.

Item 6: "How has divorce changed things for you?" Role Plays

Put each of the following role-play situations on a separate card.

ROBERT: I don't think my parents' divorce changed things very much for me. They were always too busy to spend much time with me anyway. I still go to the same school. And I still have the same friends. And there's my dog. Still the same old dog.

SUSAN: Well, I'd say things are different for me. I used to be a pretty happy person. Now I always feel as if I had done something wrong. Somehow I feel it is my fault that my parents divorced. Daddy was always yelling at Mama about how much everything cost. She yelled back that it wasn't her fault. Maybe they didn't have to spend so much on me. Maybe if I hadn't asked for a bike when I did, things would have been different.

ELAINE: Me? I don't think much about the divorce one way or the other. I don't really care what my parents do.

JERRY: Yes, things are different for me. I have to live with my mother all the time. She won't let my dad come over but once a week. I used to think she was so nice to me, but now she is so mean. Always telling me to do this or to do that. I wish I could go live with my dad. I'll bet you he would treat me right.

BARRY: I don't know how much divorce has changed me for now. But when my parents first got their divorce, I got sick. My stomach hurt all the time, and I couldn't eat anything and keep it down. The doctor said I was just upset about the divorce. But finally I got better. Only sometimes when I think about how things used to be, I still get sick.

JANE: Well, I don't know. I mean that sometimes I think things have changed a lot. And then I think they haven't changed. Sometimes I get to hoping my parents will remarry, and then I think they really will. But I know they won't. Some days I feel like crying and crying, but there are times when I don't even care. I don't know how to answer the question.

BILL: I think my father really let us down. No man ought to be allowed to just walk out and leave his family. Now that the divorce is final, he wants us to be with him part of the time. Well, I'm not going. I'd rather run away than to have to spend any time with him. I hate him. That's how things are changed for me because I used to love my daddy.

TONY: I guess you could say that there have been a lot of changes. My mom had to go to work after she and daddy got the divorce. But they both say that they still love me. And they try to be real good to me. I believe that if they both love me and if I keep on loving them—well, one day they're just sure to get married again. That's what I believe. I really do.

Item 7: Face Masks

You will need one face mask for each of the eight role-play parts. The illustrations will give you ideas for creating the masks. An alternate approach is to use puppets.

Item 8: "They Felt This Way" Strips

Manuscript write each of the following statements on separate pieces of sentence strip.

Was angry at the parent who left

Believed parents would remarry

Was physically ill

Acted indifferent

Felt guilty

Pretended nothing was changed

Was confused

Was angry with parent at home

Item 9: "They Felt This Way" Matching Chart

Prepare an individual copy of this worksheet for each pupil.

They Felt This Way

Remembering the situations which were presented, draw a line from the child's name to the response which best describes him or her.

CHILDREN	RESPONSES
Susan	Was angry at the parent who left
Robert	Believed parents would remarry
Elaine	Was physically ill
Barry	Acted indifferent
Jane	Felt guilty
Bill	Pretended nothing was changed
Tony	Was confused
Jerry	Was angry with parent at home

Item 10: Open-End Stories

Type each of these stories on a 4″ x 6″ card, using both sides of the card if necessary.

Story 1

Neal's younger sister was the kind of baby whom everyone loves. Sometimes Neal got tired of hearing people talk about how cute and sweet she was.

Most of the time he just went to his own room. He had a lot of toys there he liked to play with. Unlike some children, he was pretty particular with his toys. He took care of them and had a place for each one.

As Jeanie got bigger, she learned to crawl, and then she learned to walk. Sometimes she came into Neal's room and wanted to play with his toys. But he always told her no. Then he pushed her gently out of the room and shut the door. Neal decided he would always shut the door to his room when he wasn't going to be in it.

One day Neal forgot. When he came back to his room, Jeanie had been there. Every toy he owned was on the floor. Some were broken. When Neal saw what had happened, he . . .

Story 2

If there was anything which Kevin hated to do, it was to take out the garbage. He didn't care if some boys thought it was sissy to help in the kitchen. He would rather wash dishes, even pots and pans, or help cook a meal than to have to collect the trash from all the wastebaskets and add them to the garbage to be taken to the alley.

When household chores were assigned and Kevin sometimes got the chore of taking out the garbage, he always managed to trade out with one of his brothers or his sister who did not mind the job as much as he did.

One day his brother Robbie, who had agreed to swap jobs, forgot to carry out the garbage. Kevin was just coming in the kitchen door where his mother was hurrying to prepare supper.

"Kevin," she said, "how about gathering up the trash and garbage and getting it out to the can?"

For a moment Kevin just stood there, thinking about Robbie. Then he . . .

Story 3

"Susie," Daddy called from the doorway, "I've got to go now. I meant to help you get the living room cleaned up today. Can you do it without me?"

"Oh, bother," Susie snarled under her breath. Then she tiredly said, "Yes sir."

After she listened to her records for a while, she turned on the TV. While she was watching a cartoon, the phone rang.

"Susie, it's Jody. My folks are going to the park in about an hour. Can you go?"

Susie was delighted. But when she got home, she had only a half hour to run the vacuum, dust, pick up papers—everything. So she dusted only the surfaces that showed and ran the vacuum only down the middle of the room and stuffed the papers into the magazine rack.

When Daddy came home, he looked at the room. "Susie, did you or did you not clean this room?" he wanted to know.

Susie began to turn red, and she . . .

Story 4

Mrs. Stone must have been in a hurry when she got to school. She was just picking up her things from Todd's desk where she had set them while she hung up her coat on the rack by the door. Todd came in just as she turned around.

"Sorry, Todd. Here you are, and my things are in your way."

"That's OK," Todd said grinning. He liked Mrs. Stone a lot.

Todd went to hang up his own coat. When he sat down at his desk, he realized that there was a sheet of paper on top of it. Turning the paper around, he could see that it was the questions for today's oral quiz.

Man! One quick look at that paper and he could make a good grade. And he needed it. Why he could even read the paper while he carried it to Mrs. Stone. She would never realize what he had done. Todd looked to make sure Mrs. Stone was not watching. Then he . . .

Story 5

Mark had really been excited when he saw the ship model in the hobby store window. He thought he had never seen anything so lovely as the clipper ship. He knew he just had to have that model.

There was just one snag: the cost. Mark's allowance did not stretch to things as expensive as the model. Since the divorce, Dad had had a lot of expenses. Even if he went to see his mother that weekend, Mark knew she didn't have the money either.

Just the same when Dad tucked him in that night, Mark told him about the model. Imagine how surprised Mark was when Dad came in with the model under his arm a few days later.

Now Mark had been working on the model for three months. What a lot of detail there was: little bitty this and little bitty that. When Mark glued the yardarm in wrong and had to do it over, he decided . . .

Story 6

Steve was really distressed. Martha and Cindy were about as angry with each other as he had ever seen them. Martha had borrowed Cindy's best sweater without saying anything to her. And she had brought it home dirty. To get even, Cindy had loaned Martha's nicest dress to a friend, and Martha needed it for her big date. When the two girls had begun to yell at one another, Mom had cried.

"What did I do wrong to have two girls who act like this?" Mom said.

Steve knew that Martha and Cindy each considered herself too grown-up to take any advice from a little brother. And he knew that they considered him little even if he was only two years younger than Cindy.

Steve thought about everything he could possibly do. Finally he decided that the best thing for him to do was . . .

Item 11: Bible Verses to Help

Prepare individual copies of this work sheet so each pupil can have a copy for his notebook.

BIBLE VERSES TO HELP

Read the situations at the top of the page. Then select at least one Bible verse to help you. Put the letter of the verse in the blank before the situation.

Situations

   __ 1. You are angry with someone in your family.

   __ 2. You feel that someone at home has treated you wrong.

   __ 3. Your parent has asked you to do something you don't want to do.

   __ 4. You feel fussy and whine a lot.

   __ 5. You do a sloppy job.

   __ 6. You are tempted to do something you know is wrong.

   __ 7. You can tell an untruth and get by.

   __ 8. A member of your family needs help.

   __ 9. You do not want to finish a job.

   __10. You feel that no one likes you.

   __11. Two members of your family are angry at each other.

Bible Verses

a. "Blessed are the peacemakers" (Matthew 5:9).

b. "Have peace one with another" (Mark 9:50).

c. "Children, obey your parents in the Lord: for this is right" (Ephesians 6:1).

d. "Thou shalt do that which is right and good in the sight of the Lord" (Deuteronomy 6:18).

e. "My mouth shall speak truth" (Proverbs 8:7).

f. "Whatsoever thy hand findeth to do, do it with thy might" (Ecclesiastes 9:10).

g. "Do all things without murmurings and disputings" (Philippians 2:14).

h. "Be ye kind one to another, tenderhearted, forgiving one another" (Ephesians 4:32).

i. "Even a child is known by his doings" (Proverbs 20:11).

j. "A friend loveth at all times" (Proverbs 17:17).

k. "Let us love one another: for love is of God" (1 John 4:7).

l. "As ye would that men should do to you, do ye also to them likewise" (Luke 6:31).

m. "He that is faithful in that which is least is faithful also in much" (Luke 16:10).

n. "Thou shalt not covet" (Exodus 20:17).

Item 12: "How Divorce Sometimes Changes Things" Wall Chart

Place each of the following statements on poster board or on newsprint. In order to space the items so that the whole group may read them easily, you may need two pieces of board or newsprint. Allow space for additions children may make.

HOW DIVORCE SOMETIMES CHANGES THINGS

Mother or Father moves out.

Mother may go to work.

A relative may help take care of the children part of the time.

The children may have to spend time in a day-care center.

The family may have less money to buy things and do things.

The parents may be angry with each other.

The children may be angry with the parents.

The children may get a new stepparent.

The family may have to move.

The children may have more chores to do at home.

The children may see one parent only from time to time.

The parent the children live with may seem tired and impatient with the children.

The children may think the divorce is their fault.

A child may be sick more often than before the divorce.

Grandparents may be sad or angry about the divorce.

Item 13: "How Divorce Has Changed Things for Me" Work Sheet

Prepare a copy for each child. When the item is used, allow each child to mark the sheet as he wishes, even though his marking may not reflect known facts nor agree with the leaders' perceptions. Be sure to allow write-in space at end.

HOW DIVORCE HAS CHANGED THINGS FOR ME

Place a check before each statement that describes how divorce has changed your life.

__My father moved out.

__My mother moved out.

__My mother has gone to work.

__My father visits me or I visit him from time to time.

__My mother visits me or I visit her from time to time.

__My grandparent or other relative takes care of me part of the time.

__I spend some time in a day-care center.

__We can't buy all the things we want.

__My parents are angry with each other.

__I have a new stepparent.

__I have moved to a different home.

__I go to a different school.

__I go to a different church.

__I have to do more chores at home.

__I am sometimes angry with my mother, more than before the divorce.

__I am sometimes angry with my father, more than before the divorce.

__I feel that I caused the divorce.

__I have more stomachaches and colds and other sicknesses than I had before the divorce.

__My grandparents are sad about the divorce.

__My grandparents are angry about the divorce.

__I don't feel that very much has changed.

__My mother gets angry with me more often now.

__My father gets angry with me more often now.

__I know some Bible verses to help me feel better about my life.

__I know God still loves me.

Some other changes are:

Item 14: Evaluation Sheet

This outline is intended to serve only as a model. An evaluation sheet should always be constructed in terms of the seminar it is intended to evaluate.

Please check the statement that best tells how you feel about the item listed in this column.	It helped me a lot.	It helped me some.	It was a waste of time.
(List here the major content areas covered.)			

The part I enjoyed doing most was_____.

The most important thing I learned was_____.

If there is another class like this, I want to be in it.   __Yes __No

The part I liked the least was_____.

I hope my friends whose parents are divorced can be in a class like this. __Yes __No

Notes

Chapter 1

1. William Hodges, Ralph Wechsler, and Constance Ballantine, "The Latent Stress of Divorce for Preschoolers," *Psychology Today,* October, 1979, p. 26.

2. Jessie Bernard, *Remarriage* (New York: The Dryden Press, 1956), p. 216.

3. U.S. Department of Commerce, Bureau of the Census, *Current Population Reports,* Series P-20, No. 311, "Population Characteristics—Household and Family Characteristics: March, 1976."

Chapter 2

1. William J. Goode, *After Divorce* (Glencoe, Illinois: The Free Press, 1956), p. 47.

2. Samuel Southard, *Religion and Nursing* (Nashville, Tennessee: Broadman Press, 1959), pp. 24-25.

3. Tom R. Baine, *Marriage Happiness or Unhappiness* (Philadelphia: Dorrance and Company, 1955), p. 115.

4. *U.S. News and World Report,* August 31, 1959.

5. Harold Myra, "Ken Taylor: God's Voice in the Vernacular," *Christianity Today,* October 5, 1979, p. 22.

6. From an address by Nicholas Hobbs, "A Day of Celebration," May 3, 1976.

Chapter 4

1. William C. Rhodes and James L. Paul, *Emotionally Disturbed and Deviant Children: New Views and Approaches* (Englewood Cliffs, N.J.: Prentice-Hall, Inc., 1978), p. 43.

2. Robert Rosenthal and Lenore Jacobson, *Pygmalion in the Classroom: Teacher Expectation and Pupil's Intellectual Ability* (New York: Holt, Rinehart, and Winston, 1968).

Chapter 5

1. Robert N. Puckett, "Ministry Experience Report, Theological and Ethical Aspects of Ministry, Doctor of Ministry Workshop" (Princeton Theological Seminary, July, 1975), p. 1.

2. Judith S. Wallerstein and Joan B. Kelly, "California's Children of Divorce," *Psychology Today,* January, 1980, p. 75.